Pacific Salmon Flies

New Ties & Old Standbys

Cecilia "Pudge" Kleinkauf

Photography by Michael DeYoung

Denali National Park, Alaska. Wonder Lake with resident trumpeter swans below Mt. McKinley.

Pacific Salmon Flies

New Ties & Old Standbys

Cecilia "Pudge" Kleinkauf

Photography by Michael DeYoung

Frank Amato
Publications

All inquiries should be addressed to:
Frank Amato Publications, Inc.
P.O. Box 82112
Portland, Oregon 97282

503-653-8108
www.AmatoBooks.com

Book and Cover Design by Mariah Hinds

Photography by Michael DeYoung
www.michaeldeyoung.com

ISBN-10: 1-57188-489-0
ISBN-13: 978-1-57188-489-3
UPC: 0-81127-00334-1

Printed in Singapore

Table of Contents

INTRODUCTION

In my 40-plus years in Alaska I've enjoyed the thrill of catching Pacific salmon countless times. Early on, before I learned to fish with a fly rod, the catching was done while fishing with a spinning rod. For over thirty years, however, it's been a fly rod that has connected me to silvers, pinks, chums, sockeye, and king salmon as well as to all the other species of fish that call Alaska home.

The challenge of matching wits with these magnificent anadromous fish never gets old, nor does my interest in the flies that are used to catch them. Spotting the fish, selecting just the right ammunition, presenting it correctly, and landing the fish are all enthralling parts of the whole equation, yet, somehow it's always the flies themselves that intrigue me the most. While I love learning about them and figuring out how to use them successfully, what I am really hooked on is tying them.

The flies for Pacific salmon aren't like most of the flies that fly-fishers use. Since these salmon have stopped feeding when they re-enter fresh water to complete their life cycle, the flies that take them do not imitate any particular food source. Therefore, fly tiers have to resort to other concepts to derive inspiration for the patterns.

Because they are not eating, returning salmon take a fly for reasons other than hunger. Biologists think that motives such as an old, ingrained instinct to chase moving prey, irritation at the repeated presentation of an object in front of them, or simply the strong territorial proclivity that salmon display as the time for spawning draws near are what accounts for many strikes. Numerous fly patterns have been developed over the years for Pacific salmon fishing that have attempted to capitalize on these various theories. I, too, consider these aspects of fly design, but create Pacific salmon patterns for other reasons as well.

As you will see reflected in many of the flies in this book, I have a tendency to focus on what I believe the attraction to different tying materials might be for the fish and the general characteristics of flies, such as weight and size that make them successful for one or the other of the five salmon species. Mostly, however, tying Pacific salmon flies, in my estimation, is really all about one's general creativity and putting it to use at the vise.

Rather than give tying instructions for each and every fly, and to avoid redundancy, I have chosen to create one section of the book that gives general coaching tips for many of the various techniques that are used in more than one of the patterns.

The book also contains information on each of the five Pacific salmon species. This should help fly-fishers new to the sport of salmon fishing become more familiar with the various propensities and idiosyncrasies of each species and why one type of fly might be more successful than another. In addition, I've provided a chart to help readers select several of the best flies from the book for each salmon species.

As with my previous three books, *Fly-fishing Women Explore Alaska, River Girls: Fly-fishing for Young Women,* and *Fly-fishing for Alaska's Arctic Grayling,* I have many others to acknowledge and thank. First and foremost, of course, are Michael DeYoung, my longtime friend and stalwart photographer, and his creative wife, Lauri, who spend endless hours crafting exceptional images that make my text come alive for the reader. Besides Mike & Lauri, the project could never have come to fruition without the expert help and advice of LuAnne Dowling, editor extraordinaire, who has been there for me in all of my book projects and who, once again, graciously agreed to help set things on the right path to success. Then, Kim Callahan at Frank Amato Publications put it all together in one outstanding package as she did earlier with my Arctic Grayling book. I've been lucky to have them all.

Les Johnson, co-author of *Fly-Fishing for Pacific Salmon II,* who welcomed many of my patterns into the list of flies in his book, first gave me the idea of putting those and others all together in a book of their own. He and other accomplished fly tiers have, mostly un-wittingly, given me ideas and inspiration for some of these creations. I thank them all.

I also have to thank various members of the Alaska Fly Fishers Club and the employees of the various fly shops in Anchorage, Alaska for their never-ending willingness to talk about flies with me, analyze new materials and their possibilities, and, at times, even try out some of my creations.

I hope that readers will also use one or more of my concoctions in their salmon fishing. Surely, as a result, someone will create a new pattern of their own that will become a classic and find a place in the fly boxes of all of us who fish for the magnificent Pacific salmon.

Best Fishes!
Pudge

The Five Species of Pacific Salmon

All five species of Pacific salmon are anadromous. They begin their life in fresh water and migrate out into salt water to mature. After a year or more at sea, they return to fresh water to spawn in the exact stream where they were born, using, biologist believe, their amazing sense of smell. This process remains one the most incredible phenomena of the natural world. Unlike their Atlantic salmon relatives, all Pacific salmon die after spawning.

Each of the five species of Pacific salmon has two names as well as other special characteristics that distinguish one from the others. King salmon, also called *chinook,* are the largest, and they are usually also the first to return to fresh water in the spring and early summer. Pink or *humpy* salmon, by contrast, are the smallest, and they typically are the second species to enter fresh water in early summer. Depending on the river, sockeye or *red* salmon return just after or even at the same time as the pinks. The chum salmon, also known as *dog* salmon because of their huge teeth, and the coho or *silver* salmon are the last to return in late summer and early fall. Run timing for different species often overlaps, giving anglers the opportunity to catch several or, at times, all five of the Pacific salmon species on the same trip. When that occurs, the fishing can be nothing short of spectacular.

Many people believe that Alaska has all five species of salmon in all of the rivers all of the time. Although some rivers do host all five species at one time or another during the summer, many more do not. In reality, you can find *some* of the salmon in *some* of the rivers *some* of the time. Some rivers produce no salmon runs at all.

Anyone planning a trip to fish for a particular species of salmon in a specific river or area is wise to check the web site of the Alaska Department of Fish and Game to determine when and where that species is present in that particular region, and to consult the department's run-timing charts and sport-fish biologists in the relevant regional office for specific information. The same applies to salmon fishing in locations other than Alaska.

Spawning and Physical Changes

Sometime on their homeward migration, all Pacific salmon stop feeding, and the physiological changes that enable them to return to fresh water begin. As much as a week or two (or even longer in the case of fish with extremely long migrations) may elapse between the time the fish reenters fresh water and spawning actually begins. During that time all Pacific salmon change in various ways in both shape and color as they move upriver towards their spawning grounds. Typically, the heads of the males become somewhat more elongated, and the teeth become more prominent. In addition:

- Kings turn a deep brownish red;
- Pinks develop the hump on their back (males have much larger humps than females) and a whitish belly;
- Sockeye turn bright red with greenish heads, and males usually develop large humps on their backs;
- Chums become whitish/brown and develop unique patterns of reddish stripes down their sides as well as fang-like teeth which earn them the nickname "dogs";
- and silvers turn dark red, with males developing a large bulb on the tip of their upper snout.

It is important for you to be able to tell the species apart while fishing, in order to comply with various fishing regulations and restrictions. Here is a quick and easy method that most anglers learn to use for identification of different salmon species:

- Kings generally have their size to identify them, but regardless of their size, they have large, irregular spots all over their backs, along their sides, and on both the top and the bottom lobes of their tail. They are also the only one of the species that has a black gum line on their bottom jaw.
- Pinks may be identified by their small size as well as by their large humped back, but since female pinks often don't show much of a hump, both sexes are usually identified by the white belly they develop while spawning.
- Sockeye often display a greenish or bluish-colored back and have small scales and no spots. They soon take on a pinkish color after entering fresh water. They are larger than pink salmon, but smaller than all the other three species.
- Chums are the easiest to identify because of the stripes along their sides that become more and more garish as the fish move toward the spawning grounds. Even when the fish are fresh in from the sea, however, you can see where the stripes will be if you look closely.
- Silvers, which may be mistaken for kings in rivers where both are present, can be identified by the large, bulb nose on the males, plus the fact that they have spots on their backs but only on the top lobe of the tail. They also have a white gum line on their bottom jaw, while a king's gum line will always be black.

To learn more about Pacific salmon, visit www.adfg.alaska.gov.

Spawning occurs for all five species with the female selecting the appropriate site and then digging a nest (also called a *redd*) for the eggs with her tail. King salmon spawning sites have larger gravel and more water flow up through the gravel than the sites used by other Pacific salmon. Pink salmon spawn closer to tidewater than most other Pacific salmon species, often in intertidal zones, because they have less body fat than the other species. Pinks pick sites about 1-3 feet in depth in fairly fast current. Sockeye salmon, which require a lake in the river systems they inhabit, may spawn in either lakes or rivers in shallow, slow-moving water or small back eddies. Chum salmon typically spawn in upwelling water that is significantly warmer than the nearby river water or use pools, tail outs, and other slow-moving water in the main stem of the river. Silvers also choose fairly shallow spawning areas with moderate flow.

Males aggressively vie for the opportunity to father the eggs the female lays and can be seen chasing and biting any rivals that approach her. When she is ready she deposits the eggs in the nest and the male simultaneously releases his milt over them. The female then uses her tail to cover the nest with gravel and proceeds to repeat the process with other males until she is exhausted. She dies soon after, as do the males.

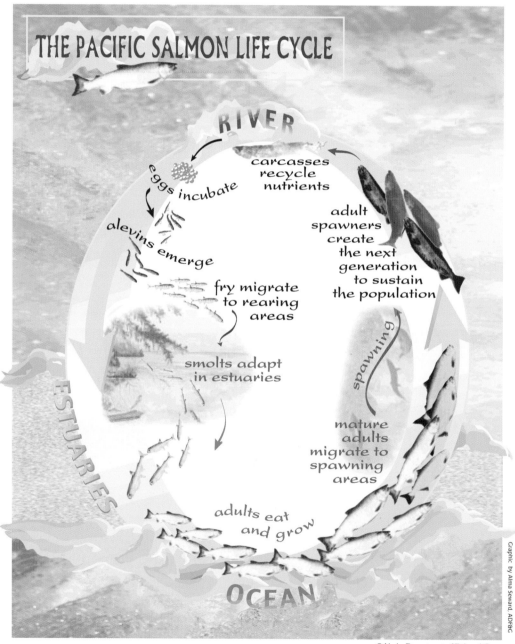

THE PACIFIC SALMON LIFE CYCLE

RIVER

eggs incubate

carcasses recycle nutrients

adult spawners create the next generation to sustain the population

alevins emerge

fry migrate to rearing areas

spawning

smolts adapt in estuaries

ESTUARIES

mature adults migrate to spawning areas

adults eat and grow

OCEAN

Graphic by Alma Seward, ADF&G

The eggs remain in the stream gravel through much of the winter. Upon hatching, the alevin hold up below the gravel and, survive off the nutrients in the yolk sac to which they are attached. As they grow into the fry stage, they emerge from the gravel and begin feeding. The immature fish reside in the freshwater river or lake for a year or more, readying themselves for a life in salt water.

The progression from fry to smolt occurs at various rates for various species, but when smoltification is complete, the little fish out-migrate to the sea. Sexually immature salmon remain at sea for one to four or five years, depending on their species. Upon reaching sexual maturity they return to the river of their birth to spawn and die. Occasionally a few sexually immature fish, referred to as *jacks* will accompany the spawners. Regardless of their inability to spawn, they, too, perish.

Fishing for Different Pacific Salmon Species

Pacific salmon are more aggressive to a fly just as they enter fresh water and for a few days thereafter, and then again as they get close to actual spawning. During the intermediate period they generally are more reluctant to strike a fly. Their concentration is on getting ready to spawn and then on spawning, and it can often be difficult to divert their attention away from that purpose. Patience and persistence are required for successful fishing, along with the use of different types and colors of flies and different stripping techniques.

Pacific salmon are not leader-shy, so it is not necessary to use delicate leaders and tippets or to worry about the salmon seeing the leader. They are so intent on their mission that nothing deters them.

It's almost always best to fly-fish for salmon by casting across and slightly down the current in order to drift the fly right into the fish's cone of vision. A couple of twitches just as it enters the strike-zone will help focus the fish's attention. It may be difficult to get a response from resting fish, but persistence, and/or a change of fly color or shape is usually worth a try to see if you can spark a response.

King (Chinook) Salmon

King salmon returning from the sea to fresh water.

King salmon are a challenging fish for a fly rod. In fact, many dedicated fly-anglers will forgo the long rod temporarily while they revert to their spin or level wind rod and a lure or bait when fishing for them.

Kings can be very large fish and heavy-duty equipment is required to handle them. A 9-, 10- or even a 12-weight rod is essential as is a quality fly reel with a top-notch drag. Leader material will depend on the average size of the fish you are targeting. Kings can be found in both large water and in smaller streams where they may be preparing to spawn. Since they are usually much larger than the other species they can often be easy to see in the water. Otherwise, blind casting may be required.

Kings are typically more aggressive to a fly just after they reenter fresh water than they are a few days later or a mile or two upstream. Still, because they are not feeding, it may be necessary to get the fly right in front of the fish, just a foot or so off the stream bottom, to elicit a strike. Large, bright flies are best used in these conditions. Farther upstream where the water may be shallower and slower, you may need smaller flies and pinpoint casting because you'll often be targeting very spooky fish. A basic drag-free drift often works with kings, as does the "hang-down" method, where the fly is just permitted to dangle in the current.

King salmon in spawning colors on the Klutina River, Alaska.

Pink (Humpy) Salmon

"Humpy" salmon are more prolific than any other salmon species in Alaska. Hundreds of thousands of them invade streams and rivers throughout the state during the summer months, and they are constant targets for the fly-fisher.

Fly-fishing for pink salmon is really quite easy. Just get a smallish pink or chartreuse fly and go to work. Because of their white bellies, pinks are very visible in even the cloudiest water, and they are the easiest of all the salmon to direct your fly toward. As the fish lie in streams almost bank-to-bank, you can spot their mouths with little difficulty. Then, you can just direct your fly to that target with fairly slow, steady strips.

Pink salmon as they enter fresh water.

Pink salmon in spawning condition.

The major problem in hooking pink salmon is that there may be so many of them in the river it becomes difficult to avoid hooking their humps as you fish. If that happens, bring the flapping fish in quickly, use your needle-nosed pliers to extract the hook, and carefully send him on his way. The other negative is that the vast majority of pink salmon that you catch in fresh water are not suitable for eating.

Having spent only one year in salt water, they have not put on a lot of weight, and their flesh deteriorates quickly once they return home. Pink salmon caught in salt water, on the other hand, have a delicate meat that most Alaskans find absolutely delicious.

In spite of their other drawbacks as a sport fish, pink salmon fight ferociously for their small size, and can provide great fun on a 6-weight rod. Learn to think of them as practice fish that you can use for learning how to manage larger fish on a fly rod or for teaching your kids how to fly-fish, and just see how much you can enjoy them. And remember, those vast amounts of fish carcasses that clog the river after spawning is over make for lots of meals for other creatures and provide vital nutrients for many, many watersheds.

Sockeye (Red) Salmon

Sockeye salmon are considered to be the middle-sized species of Pacific salmon. Not as large as cohos, kings, or chums, but not as small as pinks, they weigh on average about four to ten or eleven pounds. Someone once told me that if I was going to fly-fish for sockeye salmon I needed to remember the "S Rule." The rule, he said, was that, "sockeye, begins with an 'S' so always fish for them with flies that are small and sparse." The rule comes with the following warning, "If you wait for a sockeye to

Sockeye salmon as they enter fresh water. Before long they begin to develop the deep crimson color that characterizes them as "reds."

grab, you'll almost always go home fishless." Both were great pieces of advice, and I remember them to this day.

Sockeye salmon are unique from their cousin-species in that they feed by filtering plankton from the water rather than chasing their prey. Instead of propelling themselves toward a food particle, they just open their mouth. Since they've never chased their prey, they're generally not going to chase your fly, either. Those facts should alert you to the reality that small and sparse flies are easier to control in the water and easier to direct right to the mouth level of the fish. You may need a small split shot on the leader to help get the fly at the right depth in the water column. Once that is achieved, keeping a fairly tight line, and stripping just slightly to keep in touch with the fly as it moves along with the current, usually do the trick.

Many fly-anglers actually fish for sockeye salmon with a bare hook. They know that mastering the control of the drift is more important than any specific color or material or fly design. It's what we often call "fishsense" that alerts them to the fact that a fish has taken the fly even though they don't generally feel a thing.

Sockeye salmon fishing requires fly-fishers to be particularly focused on what their line and leader are doing in the water, and to be especially alert to when the fly simply stops in the current. The thought that you are hung up is what usually triggers the awareness that a fish has taken the fly. Often, however, that occurs when it is already too late to set the hook. Pay attention.

Sockeye salmon in spawning colors.

Chum (Dog) Salmon

Chum salmon are, without a doubt, Alaska's most underappreciated sport fish. Because their flesh deteriorates in fresh water almost as fast as pink salmon flesh, they are not considered good table fare once they enter their home stream. They are quite a desirable eating fish when caught in salt water, however.

Chum salmon are a highly challenging fly-rod fish. They average between 12 and 18 or 19 pounds, or more, of pure fight. They'll attack almost any salmon fly they encounter after which they will proceed to give the angler an amazing and challenging experience. Besides that, they are the most decorative and photo-worthy fish that swims in Alaska. Those incredible stripes and bars along their sides are unique to each and every fish. Biologists refer to them as the chum's fingerprints.

Chums especially like sparkly flies. Just tie on a bright silver or Flashabou-decorated offering and direct it right at the large, dark shape you can see holding deep in a slow-moving outside bend on the river. Suddenly your rod will feel very heavy, and the fight is on.

Chum salmon generally won't jump when you have him hooked. His fight is stubborn and deep, and he'll give you a real workout for your fishing effort. Landing chums can be as challenging as fishing for them. Their amazing strength gives them the power to make four or five or even more runs for freedom as you struggle to get them to the net. Extracting the fly from those toothy mouths makes for another super photo op. Your friends and relatives won't believe it when they see the pictures.

Chum salmon not long in fresh water.

Chum salmon in spawning condition.

Silver (Coho) Salmon

Silvers are the salmon that most Alaskans wait for all year long. Their power and acrobatics on a fly rod are unequaled by any of the other four species. They'll also chase a fly more aggressively than any of their cousins. That is why they are known as the Pacific salmon who will most eagerly take a dry fly skated on the surface if the conditions are right. The Pink Pollywog fly was invented to take advantage of this proclivity.

Silver salmon with sea lice, just entering fresh water.

A male silver salmon in full spawning glory on a river near Nome, Alaska.

Even though everyone wants to experience the excitement of seeing that large, bulb-nosed head tracking the moving fly, polliwogs, or "wogs" as fly-anglers refer to them, are not always effective. Large schools of fish in still or slow-moving water without much depth are the conditions generally required for "wogging." By far the largest numbers of fish that respond to the "wog" are males. That is thought to be due to their increasing aggression as spawning nears.

Silver salmon are the species that seem to take the widest variety of different flies and also seem to be the most affected by changes in light. They can be hitting flies with abandon just before dawn, and when the light comes on the water, the party's over. Those who love silvers acknowledge their tendency to turn on and turn off with regularity. If you pay close attention, you can see that this is almost always in response to subtle changes in light. Once they turn off, just changing to a different color fly can be the key to the "turn-on."

Lots of different fishing approaches are successful with silvers. You just have to be persistent. Probably, the basic down and across swing method takes as many fish as anything, but when it isn't effective, you need to change tactics. Dead drifting can be amazingly effective at times. Or, try retrieving with long, slow strips, hesitating occasionally to let the fly fall in the water column. Silvers will often grab it when it is sinking, just as they will grab a fly as it enters the water and begins dropping toward the bottom. Both of these takes are probably the result of the fish thinking that the fly is injured prey. Be alert for soft, almost imperceptible strikes in such situations. Even though silvers are notorious trackers and grabbers, their bite can be amazingly delicate at times.

Short, fast, popcorn strips can often take silvers when not much else is working. Don't forget that they like to chase. Mastering the two-handed strip can make the difference between getting strikes and getting skunked when fishing for silvers, especially when fishing on the surface with flies like the Pink Pollywog or Hot Lips. Look closely and you'll often see the fish dueling over your offering. (See http://www.womensflyfishing.net/ten_tips.htm#retrieve for tips on the fast strip).

Pacific Salmon Fly Characteristics and Tying Tips

Pacific salmon stop eating when they leave the ocean and reenter fresh water to return to their spawning grounds where they will mate and die. For this reason, many Pacific salmon flies do not try to imitate food sources that are important to the fish. Rather, salmon flies typically are constructed of gaudy colors and sparkly flash of one type or another simply to get the fish's attention.

Other characteristics that many Pacific salmon flies have in common are the use of extra weight to keep the fly at the fish's level in the water column, and the use of materials that have particularly good "action" in the water to help focus the fish's attention on the fly and trigger the strike instinct. Many fly tiers have also learned the benefit of using neon or fluorescent bait hooks to tie some of the salmon flies. These glow-in-the-dark hooks remained the secret of conventional anglers for many years, but are now available for fly tying. The sections that follow offer some tips for tying with extra weight and with specific hooks and materials.

Using Beads, Cones and Eyeballs

One of the newest trends in fly tying is the use of beads, cones, and eyeballs to add enough weight to the fly to reduce or eliminate the need for split shot on the leader. For many years, most of us have encouraged our flies to sink by wrapping soft lead of various weights around the shank of the hook before constructing the pattern. Together with that trick, we've now learned the value of adding additional weight to the front end of the fly by making some bright and shiny add-on an integral part of the finished product.

Beads, cones, and eyeballs can all be used to achieve additional weight while at the same time giving the flies a very realistic look and differing sink rates. Beads and cones slide right onto a hook with a flattened barb, while eyeballs are tied on on top of the hook.

A sampling of beads, cones and eyeballs.

Beads and Cones

Beads or cones can be gold, silver, brass, tungsten, plastic, glass, aluminum or baked-on enamel or other materials sized to fit different hooks. All of them come with holes drilled into them so that they slide onto the hook. To prepare the hook, however, the barb must be flattened to make insertion easier.

There are two major considerations when using beads or cones. First, the holes must be drilled specifically for fly tying so that the bead or cone slides easily around the bend of the hook. For tiers that are just starting out with beads it is important to understand that different sizes of beads fit onto different sizes of hooks. (*See the Bead and Hook Size Chart on page 20.*) A close look at the bead will reveal that one of the holes in it is smaller than the other. Typically the point of the hook will be inserted into the *smaller* of the two holes. That is also true for cones, but their shape makes it much more obvious where to insert the hook. Inserting the hook-point into the larger hole will result in the bead or cone extending down over the hook eye when it is shoved forward by the materials in the fly.

The second consideration when using beads has to do with different types or sizes of wire, and different hook eyes. It's smart to take the hook you intend to use for a particular fly into the store with you when you buy the beads or cones. That way you can try out different sizes of beads or cones to make sure that the ones you buy will slide around the bend of the hook you plan to use for the fly. Remember, when using an up-eye or bend-back hook, the hole in the bead also has to be wide enough to slide over the double wire up by the hook eye. You may have to experiment with different brands of beads or cones to find one that fits the hook you are using. Many up-eye or bend-back hooks now have tapered wire next to the eye to facilitate the use of beads and cones. Daiichi hooks are some of the easiest to use in this regard.

Beads and cones are of variable weight, so it's important to know how much weight you want to add to the fly before selecting one. Generally, the plastic and brass beads and cones provide a nice look to the fly but weigh very little. These add-ons will provide a slow sink rate for the fly. Lead or tungsten cones and beads provide much more weight for a faster sink.

Tying With Beads and Cones

Here are a few general tips to help you get started tying with beads and cones. Always be sure to flatten down the barb and place them on the hook first, and then begin to tie the fly. If you're also going to wrap lead on the hook shank, be sure to put the bead or cone on before wrapping on the lead. Often, the bead or cone slides around up at the hook eye while you work. If this becomes a problem, just position the hook in the vice with a bit of a down angle to make the bead or cone stay up against the eye.

As the fly is tied, work the body material up and into or behind the space under the cone, bead, or eyeballs as far as possible to help fill up the opening that will exist there. This helps to stop the cone or bead from sliding around. Generally, cones present this problem more often than beads. Depending on the design of the fly, consider finishing the fly by adding a hackle collar or a marabou wing to help disguise the gap that appears between the finished fly and the edges of the cone or bead.

Here is a chart that will help you determine which size of bead will fit the size of the hook that you will be using, Keep in mind, however, that various hook-bends will affect how accurate the chart might be.

Bead and Hook Size Chart

1/16"	beads fit hook sizes	22-26
5/64"	beads fit hook sizes	18-22
3/32"	beads fit hook sizes	16-18
7/64"	beads fit hook sizes	14-16
1/8"	beads fit hook sizes	12-14
5/32"	beads fit hook sizes	10 - 12
3/16"	beads fit hook sizes	6 - 8
7/32"	beads fit hook sizes	2 – 4

Eyeballs

Eyeballs may be bead chain, lead, tungsten, plastic, brass, aluminum or other materials. They add both weight and visual simulation to the fly. Of course, there are also past-on-eyes that are used primarily in saltwater fly tying. Besides simply providing more weight, many tiers believe that eyeballs can also add more realism to the fly.

The original eyeballs that most tiers learned to use were the bead-chain variety. While those did indeed add lifelike quality to various patterns, they provided minimal weight. More recently, lead eyes of different styles have been available to add weight. Lead eyes have another advantage in that they are made with a greater distance between the two eyeballs, providing extra space that enables you to create an eyed-egg with different colored chenille heads. The Starlight leech, included in this book, has that type of eyes and head. With the wide variety of eyeballs now on the market, you can select one or the other based on both the amount of weight and the look that you want on the finished fly.

Tying With Eyeballs

Whereas beads and cones just slide onto the hook, eyeballs must be tied on. Many people report that they can never get the eyeballs tied on securely and that the eyeballs always seem to rotate around their hook. So, here are a few hints to help you master this essential skill.

- Always use eyeballs that are in proportion to the hook.
- Be aware that the heavier and larger the eyeballs are, the longer it will take to tie them on securely
- Tie on the eyeballs before tying any other part of the fly so that you can position them just where you want them instead of trying to leave the right amount of space and tie them in as you finish the fly.

Follow these steps for tying on eyeballs:

1 Lay down a thread base for the eyes up close to the hook eye, and position them on top of that base. (If using an up-eye hook, lay the thread base on top of the double wire too.)

2 Next, hold the eyeball that is *closest to you* in the fingernails of your nondominant thumb and index finger and make 10 or 12 thread wraps under the hook and around the eyeball that is the *farthest away from you*, binding down that eyeball.

3 Now, hold the eyeball that is *farthest away from you* as it lies on the hook shank in the fingernails of your non dominant thumb and index finger, and make 10 or 12 thread wraps under the hook and over the eyeball that is closest to you, binding down that eyeball as well.

4 Once the eyeballs are set, begin to make figure-eight wraps over one eyeball and back under the hook, and then over the other eyeball and back under the hook until you have made at least 20 wraps. Then make several wraps over each individual eyeball again.

5 Now, make 6 or 8 wraps in front of the pair of eyeballs, and 6 or 8 wraps in back of the pair of eyeballs until the eyes are securely on the hook.

6 If the eyes still are not completely secure, repeat the figure-eight wraps interspersed with wraps over each individual eyeball until the eyes do not move.

7 If the eyes you are using enable you to tie material around the eyes, as with the Starlight Leech, this is the time to do that.

8 Whip finish behind the eyeballs to secure them before tying the rest of the fly.

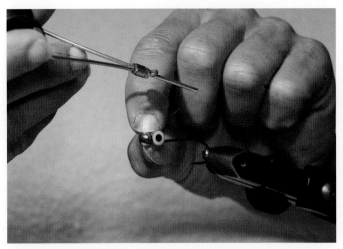
Hold closest eyeball and wrap around opposite eyeball first.

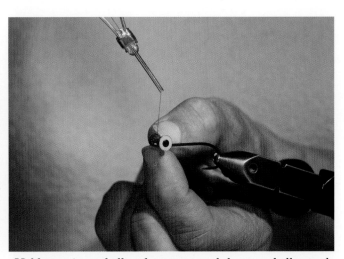
Hold opposite eyeball and wrap around closest eyeball second.

Tying a fly to a hook that already has eyeballs attached is not difficult. You can wrap lead on the hook shank for additional weight right up behind the eyes. Then, just plan to work the materials of the fly up as close behind the eyeballs as possible to help avoid the gap that often appears there when using beads and cones. Adding a hackle collar or marabou wing will also help give the fly a more finished look.

Always finish a fly that has eyeballs *behind the eyeballs* rather than in front of them. Generally, there won't be sufficient room to finish ahead of the eyes anyway, but don't take the risk of covering up the hook eye and preventing insertion of the leader.

People often ask if a fly with eyeballs will ride with the eyeballs on the underside of the hook instead of on top of the hook when it's finished. Generally, that will not occur unless the fly is fished dead drift. Most of the time, stripping the fly in the water takes care of the problem and keeps eyes on top of the fly. You'll notice that for flies where the tier wants the hook to ride up instead of down, the eyes are actually tied on the hook with the point turned up instead of turned down.

Casting Flies with Beads, Cones and Eyeballs

Besides varying the sink rate, heavier or lighter cones, beads, or eyeballs will also affect the way that the fly casts. As you might guess, the heavier they are, the harder they will be to cast. Casting heavy flies requires a somewhat slower casting rhythm and a more open loop. (Getting hit in the back of the head with one of these leaded-eyeball flies is *not* fun.) Since the extra weight of the add-on will unbalance the casting stroke, it is also important to make firm, deliberate stops on both the front and back casts.

A time-honored recommendation when casting flies with beads, cones, or eyeballs (or with the split shot you may have been using to get your fly down) is to "wait for the bounce" before beginning each forward or back cast.

There you have it. You'll quickly learn that tying with beads, cones and eyeballs adds a completely different dimension to your flies and to your fishing.

Casting flies with beads, cones and eyeballs requires
specialized techniques depending on their weight.

Tying With Glow-in-the-Dark Neon or Fluorescent Hooks

Many salmon flies that can be tied with a short-shanked hook will benefit greatly from the use of colored or glow-in-the-dark or fluorescent hooks. Daiichi's, Mustad's, and Gamakatsu's red octopus hooks are already a standard for several different patterns, but the fluorescent hooks greatly expand the range of possible colors.

Gamakatsu makes fluorescent octopus hooks that include the following:

#02607-OR	Orange fluorescent	size 8-3/0
#02608-P	Pink fluorescent	size 8-3/0
#02609-C	Chartreuse	size 8-3/0
#02610-FR	Fluorescent red	size 8-3/0
#02611-GL	Glow-in-the-dark	size 8-3/0

Mustad makes the following Neon Beak hooks:

#92569NP-CH	Chartreuse yellow
#902569NP-FC	Flame chartreuse

Besides using the Neon or glow-in-the-dark hooks, your flies can also benefit from glow-in-the-dark Flashabou, Krystal Flash, threads, and other materials that are now on the market in different colors.

Materials That Give Action to the Fly

Fly tiers know that the materials used to construct a fly are chosen because they have certain characteristics that contribute to the realism of the fly or its movement in the water. In the case of Pacific salmon flies, the issue of durability is also a factor. For those reasons and more, rabbit or bunny strips of various colors and length are used in many of these flies as are webby saddle hackle or schlappen feathers.

Tips for Using Bunny Strips

Rabbit or bunny strips become bodies, tails, and Zonker strips on various Pacific salmon flies. Although they always seem to leave tiny, furry, almost invisible remnants on my face and up my nose, I love to tie with them. The following tips will guide you in using them effectively.

Straight-cut bunny strips come in lots of colors.

Palmer the bunny strip tightly along the hook shank with the skin side down.

All that is needed to create the basic bunny fly is a strip of hot chartreuse, fuchsia, orange, purple, white, or other color of straight-cut rabbit fur. The only difficult part of tying with bunny is to remember that *your thread won't adhere to the fur, only to the skin, so the skin side of bunny must always lie against the hook.* Begin by determining which way the fur was going when it was on the bunny. Wet your fingers and stroke the bunny strip to see when the fur lies flat. Then, to create a tail, measure off an inch or more of the tip of the fur strip, and separate the fur by moistening it on both sides and pulling it apart until the skin shows through. Tie in that part of the strip just before the bend of the hook with the skin side down. The remainder of the strip is then pulled taut and palmered along the hook up to the hook eye with the skin side remaining down during the entire process. Don't place your wraps side by side or the fur on the fly will become too dense, and will not absorb water. Wide, sprailed wraps result in a more effective fly.

Most tiers have tied Zonker flies for their lake fishing, except with a feather instead of fur. But bunny strips make excellent Zonker strips as well. Begin as above by creating the tail. Don't cut off the remainder of the bunny strip. Next, create the body of the fly with your material(s) of choice, and then pull the bunny strip over the top of the body, Zonker-style, and tie it in behind the bead or cone or eyeballs.

Tips for Using Webby Saddle or Schlappen Hackle

Webby saddle or schlappen hackles are feathers whose base is wide, with fibers that stick together in small clumps and often appear oily. They are used in several different ways on Pacific salmon flies, one of the most common being as the legs on basic Woolly Buggers. The other use to which I put many of my webby saddle hackle, however, is for hackle collars. Tying the feather in by the butt up in the front of the fly gives it a completely different look. As you will come to see when you begin using beads, cones and eyeballs on your flies, there is often a visible gap between the end of your fly and the edge of the bead, cone, or eyeballs. Adding a hackle collar fills that gap but also provides long, undulating materials to rise and fall in the current as the fly is fished.

Webby saddle hackle feathers are very wide at the base of the feather.

Tying Hackle Collars

Follow these steps in tying a hackle collar:

1. Select a webby saddle-hackle feather and strip the fuzzy material off its base.
2. Tie in the feather by the stem just behind the bead, cone, or eyeballs. The right side of the feather should be facing you and the fibers should extend just about the length of the shank.
3. Being careful not to let the feather twist, closely wrap the saddle-hackle feather around right in front of the bead, cone, or eyeballs three or four times, fluffing the fibers back before each subsequent wrap. The hackle will separate in small clumps that sweep towards the rear of the hook.
4. Clip the stem and tie off.
5. As you make the head and whip-finish the fly, be sure that the hackle fibers lay back rather than pointing up dry-fly style. If necessary, stroke the fibers back, hold them down, and make one or two careful thread wraps just over the edge of them to force them to sweep back and stay there.

Collars needn't be the same color as the fly. Contrasting colors on hackle collars can add extra jazz and extra visibility to the fly. You'll likely find yourself using them a lot.

Don't let the saddle-hackle feather turn while wrapping a hackle collar.

Tangle Lakes area of the Alaska Range off Denali Highway.

Pacific Salmon Fly Patterns

Introduction to the Flies

The flies in this book are but a small, representative sample of the hundreds, if not thousands, of flies that are used to catch Pacific salmon throughout the United States. It is not meant to be a definitive collection of recommended flies, nor is it meant to suggest that there are no other effective patterns out there in the fly-fishing world.

It is simply my hope that these flies will intrigue other tiers and, perhaps, broaden the horizon of those who would fish for salmon. As the book title suggests, some of the flies are those that almost every salmon fly-angler will recognize immediately, while other are adaptations or modifications of flies I have seen, tried, read about, or been told about. And, then, there are my own creations, which I offer in the spirit of camaraderie that both fly tying and fly-fishing embody.

EVERGLOW FLY

The Everglow fly has been in use for Pacific salmon around Alaska and the Northwest in one form or another for many years. Early efforts to determine which flies in which colors were effective in catching king (chinook) salmon (especially in silty glacier rivers) resulted in clear evidence that a chartreuse fly outperformed all other colors. So, while the Everglow material is now made in both orange and pink, the predominant color for the fly is still chartreuse.

Fishing techniques for the Everglow depend somewhat on how heavily the fly is weighted. Lead on the hook shank, a bead or cone head, lead or other types of eyeballs all affect the drift and the action of the fly. Usually, the heavier the fly, the more aggressively it needs to be fished. When fishing in glacier-fed streams, do your best to get the fly right in the fish's cone of vision to help make sure that the fish can see it clearly.

While the Everglow can be fished dead-drift, an occasional twitch or short strip will help it to come alive in

the water. Keep in mind the "jigging" effect that the weighted head can have when stripped correctly. Because most Pacific salmon like to chase a fly, long, steady strips frequently induce a follow and a take. This is my favorite way to fish this fly. Its glow-in-the-dark material produces a definite, fish-like flash of light under water that other fish really respond to, so don't be afraid to strip it quickly.

Hook
Daiichi 2546 or X-point x452 or x472 or Mustad 92569 NP-CH or NP-FC Neon Beak Hook (size, 1-4) weighted or un-weighted, and with barb flattened to facilitate the use of a bead or cone

Bead/Cone/Eyes
As desired for weight and appearance and attached before tying the body of the fly

Thread
UNI-thread 6/0 chartreuse

Tail
Tips of chartreuse Everglow tubing

Body
Small chartreuse chenille wrapped around the hook shank with hollow, fluorescent Everglow tubing pulled over a weighted or unweighted body

Wing
Four strands of fluorescent glow-in-the-dark chartreuse Flashabou and four strands of pearl glow-in-the-dark Flashabou about as long as the hook shank

Collar
Webby chartreuse saddle hackle tied in by the butt and wrapped as a collar

A place to rest on the Kenai, a great salmon river.

BUNNY-WINGED SALMON LEECH

The Bunny-Winged Salmon Leech came about after I saw a somewhat similar fly in one of the fly shops in Kodiak, Alaska, years ago. I was intrigued by the long, sparkly fibers on the material called Polar Chenille that was used to tie the fly. I bought some and began tying with it, but soon discovered that the material didn't really make a bulky enough body for my tastes. So, I began experimenting. The Zonker-style use of the bunny strip pulled over two or even three layers of the Polar Chenille created a much better-looking fly, I thought. Then I also began to wrap the chenille around a set of eyeballs, added a hackle collar, and the result is what you see here.

Fishing the BWSL is much like fishing other Pacific salmon flies. I experiment with long, slow strips; quick short and fast strips; and even a near dead-drift with hardly any strips at all to see what gets the fish's attention. The bunny tail and fur give the fly a good silhouette, and, I've come to realize that the chenille-wrapped eyeballs are a definite attraction.

Tie the flies in a variety of sizes, and combine various colors if you wish. A pink body with purple bunny is a great combo, as is a white body with various contrasting colored bunny.

Hook
Daiichi 2441 (size 4 and 2) weighted, and with the barb flattened to facilitate the use of beads or cones

Thread
UNI-thread 6/0 in color to match the other materials

Eyes/Cone/Bead
As desired for weight and appearance and attached before tying the body of the fly. Can be lead, bead chain, or plastic

Tail
1 1/2-inch tip of a straight-cut bunny strip tied with the skin down against the hook, with remainder left attached to create the body

Body
Orange, fluorescent green, or fuchsia Polar Chenille to match the bunny color and wrapped from head of the fly to rear and back again for bulk

Wing
The remainder of the bunny strip used to form the tail, pulled forward to just behind the eyes like a Zonker strip

Collar
Webby saddle hackle to match the color of the tail and the body tied in by the butt and wrapped as a collar

A bright, healthy silver salmon from a remote river in Prince William Sound, Alaska.

LITTLE RED RIDING

When creating fly patterns for salmon I love to put materials together in different ways, see what the results look like, and then go try them out on a fishing trip. Such was the way the Little Red Riding came about. Knowing that the color red was often a "trigger" color for a strike from a salmon in clear water, I got to wondering what an entirely red fly might do. Since I already knew the lure of marabou to most of the Pacific salmon species, I decided to start with that. Tying it fluffing out all around a short-shanked hook, proved to be a good start. The need for weight, however, spurred me on to try beads, cones, and eyeballs. When I finally got the inspiration to wrap red chenille around red Presentation eyes tied on in front of red marabou on a red hook, things really got hot. To finish it off, I've now added a few strands of red Flashabou plus a red hackle collar, and off we go to grandmother's house on the river.

Because there is no weight on the shank of the hook, the Little

Red Riding is most definitely a jig-like pattern. Fishing with an up-and-down jigging motion in front of a reluctant silver, king, or chum salmon usually does the trick. Don't hesitate to strip this fly as well. Short and jerky is a way that works for me, but if that doesn't do the trick, use the tried-and-true long, slow strip.

Hook
Daiichi 2553 red octopus hook, or Gamakatsu fluorescent red bait hook 02610-FR (size, 2, 1, or 1/0) un-weighted

Thread
Red UNI-thread 6/0

Eyes
LG or XL lead eyes, LG red Presentation Eyes, LG gold or nickel eyes, or XL bead-chain eyes

Body
Red marabou with a few strips of red Flashabou

Head
Red chenille wrapped around the eyeballs

Wing
Red, gold or silver Flashabou

Collar
Webby red saddle hackle tied in by the butt and wrapped as a collar

Casting away in the salmon ponds at Cordova, Alaska.

FLASH FLY

True to its name, the silver and red Flash Fly is meant to be simply that, flashy. It's big and bright and attention-getting. Often, that is all you need to interest Pacific salmon, especially if they are silvers and kings. Salmon anglers tie this fly in sizes up to 1/0 for silvers, and even to 3/0 and 4/0 for kings. Although it usually works best in fishing locations near tide water or just a short distance upriver, it can be useful anywhere salmon are found.

The darting, fleeing motion of the strip is what makes the Flash Fly perform best. It doesn't have to be a perfect imitation of the real thing; it just has to reflect quick movement in the water. A fast, two-handed strip of this fly, such as the one used in saltwater fly-fishing, seems to excite the salmon most quickly. Silver salmon, particularly, are chasers. They'll follow a stripped fly almost to your feet before grabbing, or, to your disappointment, turning away. The faster I strip, the quicker I seem to be able to convince them that they need to snatch the fly before it gets away. Still,

you'll often be surprisingly successful with the Flash Fly if you just let it drop through the water column in front of waiting fish like injured prey.

Don't forget that at times, the Flash Fly can be too flashy. Just tie up a few in smaller sizes or other, darker color combinations and see what happens. Some of my favorite alternative combos are blue and green, and purple and gold.

Hook
Daiichi 2546 or X-point x452 or x472 (size, 4-2) weighted or un-weighted and with the barb flattened to facilitate the use of a bead or cone

Thread
UNI-thread 6/0 red

Bead/Cone/Eyes
As desired for weight and appearance and attached before tying the body of the fly

Tail
Silver or red Flashabou

Body
Red or silver Diamond Braid

Under Wing
Several strands of red bucktail (optional)

Over Wing
Silver and/or red Flashabou

Collar
Webby red saddle hackle tied in by the butt and wrapped as a collar

Stringing up for salmon fishing in bear country.

FISH CANDY

No matter how you look at it, there's no better fly for Pacific salmon than Fish Candy. It's about as simple a fly as you could want, and yet is unbelievably effective. Just a few wraps of the glittery material called Cactus Chenille on a short-shanked hook is all you need to catch any of the five salmon species. Just vary the color and the size, of the hook. Both the smallest and the largest of the Pacific salmon (kings and pinks) definitely prefer hot pink, with chartreuse a close second. Hot pink is also the favorite color for sockeye salmon, the hardest of all the Pacific salmon to catch. Silvers will take both colors but also turn on to hot orange, purple, and even white in different light conditions, as do chums.

Keep the flies you plan to use for pinks and sockeyes small, perhaps a size 6 but keep increasing the size, of the hook to the #4 or #2 ranges as you fish for silvers and chums, and to #2/0 or #3/0 hooks for kings. Cactus Chenille comes in several different sizes to correspond with different hook sizes. The fly can be effective on anything from a dead-drift to a super-fast retrieve. Pink salmon seem to like them bounced just off the bottom, and sockeye inhale them drifting at mouth level.

Jazz up your Fish Candy flies with embellishments like eyeballs, beads, cones, sparkly tails and wings, bunny tails and Zonker strips, hackle collars, or wispy marabou tails and wings sporting a few strands of Krystal Flash or Flashabou. Cactus Chenille is a material just begging for innovation.

BASIC

Hook
Mustad 7970 or Daiichi 2553 red octopus hook (size 6-2) weighted or un-weighted, and with the barb flattened to facilitate the use of a bead or cone when tying the Beyond Basic versions

Thread
UNI-thread 6/0 in color to match the fly

Body
Any bright color or white Cactus Chenille wrapped along a weighted or un-weighted hook

BEYOND BASIC

Hook, Body, and Thread
Same as Fish Candy basics

Eyes, bead, cone
Bead chain, lead, or plastic as desired for differing sink rate and appearance and attached before tying the body of the fly

Tail and Wing
Fluffy marabou about as long as the hook shank, in the same or contrasting color as the Cactus Chenille, plus three or four strands of multi-colored Krystal Flash, or, as a variation, a dozen or so strands of single or multi-colored Krystal Flash or Flashabou about as long as the hook shank

Collar
A very webby saddle hackle the same color as the tail or body tied in by the butt and wrapped as a collar

RAJAH

The Rajah is a pretty little fly, pleasing to the eye of both the angler and the fish. Originally created for steelhead, as the story goes, this fly has earned a place in the fly boxes of many Pacific salmon fly-anglers as well. Simple to tie, it meets the criteria for a small and sparse fly for sockeye. Silvers are also known to take it eagerly. The fly is usually fished a bit differently for these two species.

Very seldom does a sockeye salmon chase a fly. Having grown up feeding mostly by filtering plankton out of the water, they are thought not to have developed the chase instinct common to other salmon species. An aggressively stripped fly seldom brings a strike. If, however, your fly is lightly weighted or unweighted and fished so that it drifts downstream just at the fish's mouth level, you'll often get a take. A fly like the Rajah makes that easier to achieve than do the larger and heavier salmon patterns. But be ready to strike whenever the drift just stops or hesitates briefly.

Fishing the Rajah for silvers is often successful with that same slow drift, but can also trigger explosive, slamming

strikes when stripped quickly in the top part of the water column among a good pod of resting fish.

Usually the Rajah is not tied with lead on the hook shank, but at times some anglers do tie it with a bead head on heavy salmon fly hooks for just a bit more weight. The most commonly used color seems to be pink, but I know some who swear by the chartreuse version and use nothing else.

Hook
Daiichi 2441 (size 6-2) un-weighted

Thread
UNI-thread 6/0 black, pink or green to match fly color

Tail
Fluorescent pink or green bucktail to match fly color

Body
Silver tinsel or Diamond Braid for rear 2/3 of the hook and then fluorescent pink or green chenille for the egg

Wing
White bucktail, calf tail, or polar bear

Collar
Webby fluorescent pink or green saddle hackle tied in by the butt and wrapped as a collar

A pair of sockeye salmon heading upstream to spawn.

PURPLE EGG SUCKING LEECH

It may really be true that, "you can fish Alaska with just one fly in your fly box." The Egg Sucking Leech is truly found everywhere in Alaska, on every stream or river being used for every one of the five different species of Pacific salmon, and for many other species of fish as well. Tied large or small, with plain or Cactus Chenille, with a salmon-colored chenille head or a hot-orange plastic bead head, it's an ever-present fly in everyone's fly boxes. Nobody can explain exactly what it is about this fly that makes it so effective. It just is. Laughingly said to imitate, "*a leech eating a salmon egg,*" it's supposedly imitating two favorite fish foods at the same time.

In addition to the traditional purple, experimentation over the years has proven that orange, black, olive, hot pink, hot chartreuse, or even white ESLs readily catch fish. Most anglers tie various sizes of ESLs as well as different colors. They may have a box full of size 8 or 6 for the rainbows, char, and Arctic grayling that hang around the spawning salmon, size, 4 for the pinks and sockeye, 2 and even 1/0 for silvers and chums, and up to 2/0 and 3/0 for kings.

It always seems to me that there is really no wrong way to fish this fly either. Stripping, drifting, twitching, jigging, swinging all work at various times for one or the other of the five Pacific salmon species. Try different techniques to find what is working on that particular stream on that particular day. Just be sure that you also have some smaller, sparser flies in your box, particularly if it's pink or sockeye salmon you are after.

Hook
Daiichi 2441 (size 4-2/0) usually weighted

Thread
UNI-thread 6/0 in color to match the other materials

Tail
Fluffy marabou with several strands of rainbow Krystal Flash

Eyes
Optional; if used, wrap egg material around them

Body
Medium chenille or Cactus Chenille wrapped ¾ of the way down the hook shank

Hackle
Webby saddle-hackle feather tied in by the tip at the hook-bend and palmered 3/4 way down the shank on top of the chenille

Egg
Salmon, fuchsia, chartreuse, or bright orange chenille tied in on the last ¼ of the hook to form an egg in front of the body and right behind the hook eye. The egg can be tied on the hook prior to making the remainder of the fly if you prefer.

Here he comes on an Egg Sucking Leech.

Silver (coho) salmon fishing in small streams of eastern Prince William Sound, near Cordova, AK.

SOCKEYE ORANGE

Because sockeye (red) salmon don't "grab," the angler needs to be extra sensitive to what the leader is doing as the fly moves through the water. The tiniest movement or hesitation of the line can signal a take, and a fast reaction is required in response. Often the leader just stops as though the fly is hung up. Nope, that's probably a fish, with your fly in its mouth. Wait just a second too long, and the fish has ejected the fly before you've had time to set the hook. Flies like the sockeye orange meet the S-Rule criteria of small and sparse, which helps the angler to control the fly at all times.

Being able to constantly feel what the fly is doing is the key to successful sockeye fishing. That means keeping a fairly taut line and concentrating on your leader to the exclusion of everything else. Some recommend fishing sockeye with long leaders and dead-drifts, but I believe that enables the fish to take the fly for a few seconds and spit it out before the angler even knows that a fish might be on the line.

I prefer a short leader, maybe six to seven feet or so, with a fly like the sockeye orange, fished at times almost as though the angler was nymphing. The success of flies like the Sockeye Orange result from the angler's understanding of the techniques that are necessary for facilitating and recognizing a take. One of my friends very successfully fishes sockeye with a bare hook, having learned that it really isn't just the fly, but the highly developed awareness of when the fish has the hook in its mouth that makes the difference.

Hook
Daiichi 2441 (size 2-6) weighted or un-weighted

Thread
UNI-thread 6/0 black or orange

Eyes
Optional, bead chain, lead, or plastic

Tail
Black squirrel or calf tail, optional

Body
Flat silver tinsel or silver Diamond Braid wrapped down the hook shank

Wing
Black squirrel or calf tail tied under or on top of the collar

Collar
Fluorescent orange saddle hackle tied in by the butt and wrapped as a collar

Fly-fishing for sockeye salmon on Kodiak Island, Alaska.

LEMON FLY/FUCHSIA-FUCHSIA

The original name of the Lemon Fly is pretty much lost in Alaska's fly-fishing lore. Created and fished by a fellow whose last name was Lemon, it has come to be known simply as the Lemon Fly. Because one of our favorite versions of this little fly is two different fuchsia-colored materials, it is also known to many as the Fuchsia-Fuchsia.

Like other small, sparse sockeye flies, the Lemon Fly is easy and quick to tie. Consisting of only two materials, it creates a fly that meets every criteria of the 'S' Rule. Its hook is usually a short-shanked red or even fluorescent white or green in size 6 or 4, and its sparse materials consist of just Glo-Bug yarn and a bright little tail of either Krystal Flash or Flashabou.

The fishing techniques using the Lemon Fly for sockeye salmon are identical to those of flies like the Sockeye Orange and others. A fairly short leader with a tiny split shot if necessary to get the correct depth, slow strips, and an intense sensitivity to the behavior of the line and the leader as the fly drifts along, do the trick.

Many people like the Lemon Fly

because it provides the opportunity for innumerable combinations of colors and materials. The Glo-Bug yarn can be anything from deep fuchsia to chartreuse green, or hot pink, to bright red, and the tail of Flashabou or Krystal Flash can either match the specific color or contrast drastically. I'm particularly wild about the fuchsia yarn head and fuchsia Flashabou body, and I like the glow-in-the-dark Flashabou with chartreuse head too.

Hook
Mustad 7970 or Mustad 92567R or the 92569NP-CH or NP-FC Neon Beak Hook (size 4-2) un-weighted

Thread
UNI-thread 6/0 in color to match the fly

Wing
Fifteen or 20 strands of multicolored or solid-colored Flashabou or Krystal Flash tied in ¼ inch behind the eye and extending about ½ inch beyond the bend of the hook

Head
Small clump of Glo-Bug yarn in bright orange, hot pink, or chartreuse, to match or contrast with the wing, tied in right behind the eye and brushed to fuzz it out.

A successful sockeye salmon fishing day on the Kvichak River, Alaska.

BEAD-HEAD ELECTRIC LEECH

Really just a gussied-up Woolly Bugger, this is an old-reliable Pacific salmon fly if there ever was one. There is definitely a little something extra with this fly that silvers, especially, seem to find attractive. I'm not sure if it is the defined silhouette of the Flashabou or the bead head, or the combination that makes it work, but work it does for silvers, chums, and sometimes even kings.

Fished just like a Woolly Bugger in long, steady strips or in short strips interspersed with short pauses, the action of this fly in the water definitely attracts fish. Many anglers prefer a down-and-across presentation with a swing like a steelhead fly, and this approach, too, is effective.

The color and electricity of the Flashabou side strips seem to make a difference in different water conditions. The bright, Kelly green definitely shows itself well in murky or glacial water or low-light conditions, while the fuchsia or dark blue seem to shine best in clear, low water. And, as with other Pacific salmon flies, the weight provided by a bead or cone helps keep the fly near the bottom.

Electric Leeches are tied in many different colors, but black ones are definitely my favorites. Not only can all the different colors of Flashabou contrast well with it, but it seems to me that black is one of the universal colors that fish always respond to. Yes, Pacific salmon love the jazzy, bright colors, but never leave home without some of these dark beauties for times when the fish tire of jazz.

Hook
Daiichi 2441 (size 6-2) weighted or un-weighted and with the barb flattened to facilitate the use of the bead

Thread
UNI-thread 6/0 black or color to match the fly

Bead/Cone/Eyes
As desired for weight and appearance and attached before tying the body of the fly

Tail
Fluffy marabou with several strands of rainbow or solid-color Flashabou tied in along each side (don't cut off the Flashabou as it is needed for the body)

Body
Medium chenille (purple, black, white, etc.) wrapped along the hook with rainbow or solid-color Flashabou laid along each side

Hackle
Webby saddle-hackle feather palmered down the hook shank

Collar
Matching or contrasting color webby saddle hackle tied in by the butt and wrapped as a collar

Landing a silver salmon in a large back slough in Prince William Sound, Alaska.

STARLIGHT LEECH

A big bruiser of a fly, the Starlight Leech is one of my favorite Pacific salmon patterns. It has everything a fish would want: bunny tail, Cactus Chenille body, large, webby hackle color, and prominent eyes with one or another attractor color of chenille wound around them. What more could a fish ask for?

The Starlight Leech is tied in lots of different combinations of colors for different water conditions, although black remains the most common color for most of the pattern. A black bunny tail, preceded by black Cactus Chenille, almost always forms the body on my flies. Then, the fun starts with lead or Presentation eyes of different colors matched with the same or contrasting color chenille and hackle color. I seldom tie this fly on a hook smaller than #4, and, depending on whether I'm after kings or silvers, the hook size, might be size 2 or 1/0 or 2/0.

The Starlight Leech is one of those flies that require you to pay close attention to your casting technique. Because of its weight and size, you'll need to slow down your cast and open

your loops a little to avoid hitting your fly rod, or yourself in the head, as the fly whizzes by. Once in the water, the fly will sink rapidly and requires quick, strong strips to generate the correct action. Jigging is possible with this fly, as well, and some still prefer the long, steady stripping technique used for basic streamer-fishing. Because it will also make a big splash when it lands, this fly is best used in fairly fast and/or deep water.

Hook
Daiichi 2441 (size 4-1/0) weighted or un-weighted

Thread
UNI-thread 6/0 in color to match the body

Eyes
Dumbbell lead eyes attached to the hook before the rest of the fly is tied and wrapped with fuchsia or chartreuse sparkle chenille

Tail
1 1/2 inch-long-section of a strip of straight-cut bunny fur strip tied in skin-side down

Body
Cactus Chenille of the same or contrasting color as tail wrapped forward along the hook shank up to the eyes

Wing
Optional. The remainder of the bunny strip pulled over the body Zonker-style and tied in just behind the eyes

Collar
Webby hackle feather in a color to match the tail or body tied in by the butt and wrapped as a collar

Four-legged anglers fish the same streams we do in Alaska.

NOTHING FLY

I can't remember the original name of this fly, but most everyone now calls it the Nothing Fly because there is really nothing to it—just eyes and FisHair. I may have forgotten the name, but once I fished with it, I never forgot how well it performed for pink salmon, the fish it was designed for, plus sockeye and silver salmon as well.

Effective flies that are easy to tie are some of my favorites, and this is definitely one of them. There aren't any special tricks to this fly except to be sure to tie on the eyes well back from the hook eye so that you can construct a tarpon-like beak on the front of the hook with tying thread. Don't use any weight on the hook shank, and use just bead-chain eyes so the fly isn't too heavy. That is quite a contrast to some of the other large, heavy flies that are so successful for Pacific salmon. But, as with many of the effective sockeye flies, controlling the drift is the important.

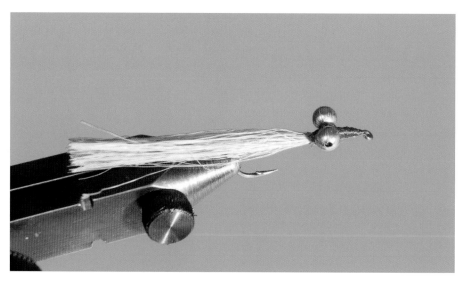

FisHair emits a definite glow under the surface of the water, and I'm convinced that is what makes the little Nothing such a good producer. I can see it and so can the fish. When using the "drift the fly right to the fish's face" technique, the Nothing does just what it is told, and usually scores. Just use a small split shot a foot or so above the fly to help regulate the depth, and time your strip to the speed of the current.

Hook
Daiichi 1720 (size, 6-2) un-weighted

Thread
UNI-thread 6/0 fuchsia or red

Wing
A clump of hot-pink FisHair tied in about 1/4 inch behind the hook eye and extending an inch or two beyond the bend of the hook

Eyes
Gold bead-chain tied in right on top of the FisHair wing with a tapered thread head constructed between the eyes and the hook eye

Pink salmon with the Nothing Fly on a stream near Cordova, Alaska.

RED HOT

You can't find a simpler fly than this one. Hook and Flashabou, that's all there is. But not just any hook nor just any Flashabou. The short-shanked, red or fuchsia, glow-in-the dark hook provides much of the appeal, and multiple strands of sizzling fuchsia Flashabou fluttering in the current are irresistible to fish.

The original version of this fly used a bright-red hook and lipstick-red Flashabou to interest the fish, but now you can also get the same great results by using the fluorescent fuchsia combination as you see here. Some anglers use Gamakatsu's chartreuse short-shanked fluorescent hook and Kelly green Flashabou with real success, too. That fly is referred to as "green eyes." Try the fluorescent orange hook and bright orange Flashabou as well.

Many people ignore unpretentious Pacific salmon flies like the Red Hot thinking that surely they can't produce fish the way the large, beefy flies do. Operating on the "big fish, big fly" theory, they bypass these small offerings all the time. When fishing for sockeye salmon, however, that decision can be a big mistake.

Remember the S Rule; Small and sparse. The Red Hot fits it to a T.

Anglers often notice that the small flies frequently catch fish just as the line straightens out. That is usually because, at least for a few moments, the fly is likely floating right at the fish's mouth before the current carries it to the surface. Learn to be extra vigilant at such times, leave your fly in the water just a second or two longer, and see if that works for you. It often does for me.

Hook
Gamakatsu red octopus, or Gamakatsu fluorescent red bait hook #02609-FR, or Daiichi 2553 red octopus (size 6-1/0)

Thread
UNI-thread 6/0 red

Wing
A clump of bright red or fuchsia Flashabou tied in right behind the hook eye and extending just past the bend of the hook

A pair of sockeye salmon about to spawn near Cordova, Alaska.

FLESH FLY/BUNNY FLY

The reliable and easy-to-tie Bunny Fly can be found in the mouths of all five species of Pacific salmon at one time or another. It's usually all about the color. Bunny just seems to have a special something in the way it moves in the water that makes it tantalizing to the fish. Tied in purple, chartreuse, or even white, with a copper bead-head, it's a real silver-getter. Tied extra-large with eyeballs or a hot red bead, it gets the attention of kings. Tying this fly with a hackle collar results in two wonderfully enticing materials moving in the water at the same time.

Bunny Flies should be carefully observed as you start to fish them because the fur may be so compact that the fly doesn't absorb water and won't sink. Some streamside snips up under the dense fur to skinny it down will be necessary to cure the problem. When tying, be careful to palmer your bunny strips at wide angles along the hook shank rather than wrapping them side by side to avoid creating these overweight flies.

The main appeal of Bunny Flies is probably the large silhouette they

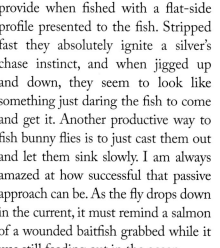

provide when fished with a flat-side profile presented to the fish. Stripped fast they absolutely ignite a silver's chase instinct, and when jigged up and down, they seem to look like something just daring the fish to come and get it. Another productive way to fish bunny flies is to just cast them out and let them sink slowly. I am always amazed at how successful that passive approach can be. As the fly drops down in the current, it must remind a salmon of a wounded baitfish grabbed while it was still feeding out in the ocean.

Hook
Daiichi 2441 (size 6-1/0) weighted or un-weighted, and with barb flattened to facilitate the use of a bead or cone

Thread
UNI-thread 6/0 in color to match the other materials

Bead or Egg-head
Salmon-colored chenille egg or gold, copper, or other colored bead, inserted on the hook before tying the remainder of the fly

Tail
1 1/2- to 2-inch tip of tan or flesh-colored straight-cut bunny strip tied in skin-side down, with several strands of Krystal Flash optional (Note: tie this fly in black, fuchsia, chartreuse, purple and other colors to interest salmon at all times.)

Legs
In same or contrasting colors, one to three sets spaced out along the hook shank and tied in as the bunny is palmered along the hook

Body
Remainder of straight-cut bunny strip palmered tightly down the hook shank with the legs tied in at intervals up to the hook eye or bead

Wing
Several strands of Krystal Flash

Collar
Same or contrasting color webby saddle hackle tied in by the butt and wrapped as a collar

Boats await a commercial fishing opening on the Ugashik River, Alaska Peninsula.

COMET

There are several flies that catch all five species of Pacific salmon, and the little unassuming Comet is one of the best. Luckily for us, it is also one of the easiest and quickest to tie. There are several variations of the Comet, some with tails of marabou, bucktail, hackle fibers or wool. Bodies can be made of tinsel, Diamond Braid, Mylar tubing, or other materials, and, while bead-chain is the most commonly used type of eyes, other types and materials will also be effective. Tiers combine these various materials almost endlessly.

Beyond the materials, I think it is the basic design of the fly that makes it so effective. Sleek and simple, with a long hackle collar that waves in the current, the fly proves especially effective on pinks, sockeye, and silvers. I particularly like orange and chartreuse for my wing and tail color, but tie this fly

on a large hook in hot pink, and you can watch the kings go after it. Don't limit yourself to just the hot bright colors, either. I have a friend who loves to tie Comets in dark green, purple and blue to good effect.

Fish the Comet dead-drift or on the swing. Both methods are effective, as are either long, slow strips or the quick movement that makes the fly dart like a baitfish. Various weights of eyeballs or lead on the shank of the hook will help put the fly at different levels in the water column as does a small split shot on the leader. Have several different colors and sizes with you for diverse water conditions.

Hook
Daiichi 2441 (size 6-1/0) weighted or un-weighted

Thread
UNI-thread 6/0 in color to match the other materials

Eyes
Bead chain, lead, or plastic as desired for weight and appearance and attached before tying the body of the fly

Tail
Fluffy marabou with or without a strand or two of Krystal Flash or Flashabou

Body
Silver, gold, or other color Diamond Braid or tinsel

Collar
A very webby saddle hackle the same color as the tail tied in by the butt and wrapped as a collar

Exploring a plunge pool for salmon in Prince William Sound, Alaska.

Alaska's Lake Clark National Park, Turquoise Lake, Telaquana Mountain.

PURPLE PERFORMER

I was guiding a group for sockeye salmon on Kodiak Island, Alaska one July when we ran out of the flies that were working. Fish were thick, and the fishing had been great, but I'd underestimated a couple of the flies that had turned out to be the most successful and, therefore, hadn't brought enough of the materials I needed to tie more. As with many flies originally tied out of desperation, I sat down that night and proceeded to experiment with what I had. That included bucktail, Diamond Braid, marabou, and saddle hackle in various colors.

Keeping in mind that sparse patterns are always the most successful with sockeye, I went to work. Needless to say, it was a late night. The next day, though, one of my creations stood out as an incredible fish-catcher, and the Purple Performer was born. I've since come to substitute squirrel tail for bucktail because I like its shine, but nothing else has changed.

The Performer is an easy fly to adjust to the speed and depth of the water. Although you can weight it to deal with deeper water or to help lessen the need for split shot on your leader, the original fly was un-weighted. If I do use eyeballs on this fly, they are almost always just bead-chain or plastic. Keep in mind that a too-heavy fly will often impede the "dead-drift at mouth level" technique that is so successful with sockeye. A fly that is too light will usually end up in the fish's dorsal fin. The Purple performer seems to fit right in between those two extremes.

Hook
Daiichi 2441 (size 6-2) weighted or un-weighted

Thread
UNI-thread 6/0 black or purple

Body
Purple or multicolor purple Diamond Braid

Under Wing
Squirrel tail or bucktail

Collar
Webby purple saddle hackle tied in by the butt and wrapped as a collar

A bright, fresh sockeye salmon from a small bay on Kodiak Island, Alaska.

FAT FREDDY

Fat Freddy has to be the weirdest looking of all the Pacific salmon flies. Despite how it looks, nobody in Alaska goes fly-fishing for king salmon without Freddie. People actually laugh when an angler pulls one of these out and ties it on the leader. When the hook-ups begin, the laughing quickly stops.

Probably created to imitate a glob of salmon eggs, which conventional anglers are so prone to attach to the treble hook on their large spoon, Freddy proves his worth when the chips are down. Tied in different sizes depending on where the king salmon fly-angler plans to fish, you'll see this fly tied in size 2 to 4/0 depending on the typical weight of the kings in a given drainage. Because the Glo-Bug yarn can be very dense on this fly, it has a tendency to sink slowly. Before fishing it, try holding it under the surface and squeezing it like a sponge to make it absorb water better.

Just as the conventional angler would do with the real egg glob, the Freddy is usually either allowed to sink and sit on the bottom or stripped slowly in front of resting behemoths. Many anglers just stand and dangle it in the water right in front of the fish's mouth. Low-water pools usually hold very spooky fish, necessitating smaller flies than the fish's size might otherwise indicate.

Hook
Mustad 34007 (size 1/0-4/0) weighted

Thread
UNI-thread 6/0 red or orange

Tail
Large clump of white marabou with or without silver Flashabou strands

Body
Six or eight strips of orange or fuchsia Glo-Bug yarn about 2 1/2 inches long and tied in tightly, one on top of the other all around the hook shank and then picked out with a bodkin and trimmed to form a large, shaggy ball

Wing
Large clump of white marabou topped with large clump of silver Flashabou strands

Beak
Long, tapered, tarpon-style head in bright orange or fuchsia (use head cement or epoxy for extra strength)

A great king salmon in early spawning colors from the Klutina River, Alaska.

POPSICLE

The absolute magic of marabou in the making of Pacific salmon flies can't be denied. Fluttering, waving, undulating, and throbbing in the current, it makes the fly come alive with movement that attracts and entices the fish to come and take a taste. George Cook's Popsicle combination of orange, pink, and purple, embellished with ivory or other colors of Flashabou, seems to make this fly totally irresistible to silver salmon.

You can create a body of silver tinsel along the hook of the Popsicle, even though the original has a bare hook for a body. I've also come to add a bead and/or a cone to the head of some of my Popsicles to provide a bit of added weight.

When I was first introduced to the Popsicle my reaction was that it was much too flimsy. I thought that it would just flatten down to nothing in the current, so I wasn't too enamored with it. Then, when one of my clients chose that fly out of a fly box that I gave her to use, and proceeded to catch six silvers in a row with it, I became a believer. I've experimented with all of the different color combinations but

have had the best success with the original and with a green-and-white cone-head version for silvers. Lots of both are always in my fly boxes.

Because of its movement in the water, you can guess that the way to fish this fly is with medium-fast strips with a pause in between to give the fly extra "poof" as it is stripped along. If you have that much movement in the fly, it's criminal not to take advantage of it.

Hook
Daiichi 2220 (size 6-1/0)

Thread
UNI-thread 6/0 black or red

Bead/Cone/Eyes
As desired for weight and appearance and attached before tying the body of the fly

Body
One clump of orange marabou with a few gold and purple strands of Flashabou or Krystal Flash wrapped to surround the hook shank. Then another clump of red marabou a little further up the hook, attached in similar fashion with additional strands of Flashabou or Krystal Flash

Collar
Purple or black marabou tufts or webby saddle or schlappen hackle tied in by the butt and wrapped as a collar

Fighting a fish on a pristine wilderness river in northwest Alaska.

BLUE SKIES

Blue Skies is another of the small, sparse flies that I tie especially for sockeye salmon fishing, even though it sometimes surprises me by ending up in the jaw of a silver or pink salmon. It is unobtrusive, even delicate, and can easily get lost in a fly box full of larger, furrier, bushier patterns. I make sure not to let that happen by always putting them on the top row of whichever box is going to transport them to the river for me.

This little fly is kind of like a secret weapon when it comes to fishing for the hard-to-hook sockeye. Keeping in mind that young sockeye were primarily plankton eaters, I tie it small to make it appear a little more like what they had been feeding on long before they reentered fresh water to spawn.

Because the word *plankton* means drifting, that is the way I fish this fly. In the water, the Blue Skies often appears as a tiny bit of flowing light drifting along in the current. Rather than absolutely dead-drifting it, though, I keep a fairly tight line in order to be able to stay aware of the fly and what it's doing. The sockeye take can be

so subtle that success requires close attention to the behavior of the line and leader at all times. Very often, the line and leader just stop. You'll think that you are stuck on the bottom, only to find a fish on the other end of the line when you pull up to dislodge the fly. Of all the Pacific salmon species, the sockeye is the one that most requires attention and concentration while fishing.

Hook
Daiichi 1701 or 1720 (size 6-4) weighted or un-weighted

Thread
UNI-thread 6/0 black

Body
Light blue tinsel or Diamond Braid, or several strands of Krystal Flash wrapped as a rope

Collar
Webby white saddle hackle tied in by the butt and wrapped as a collar

Over Wing
Several strands of blue Krystal Flash

A fresh, bright sockeye salmon from Bristol Bay, Alaska.

YARNY

When I started fly-fishing, one of the things that happened to me over and over was that someone who was catching lots of fish would tell me that all they were using was yarn. They would even show me the large wad of dripping red-orange material that seemed to lure the fish right to them. Most of them said that they thought that the material's effectiveness resulted from the fish getting the yarn caught in its teeth. Whether or not they were right, I began using yarn and caught silvers, kings, and sometimes chum. But the yarn didn't seem to be at all effective for sockeye or pink salmon.

After various fits and starts, I accepted the fact that all I really needed for an effective sockeye fly was a small amount of material. Pretty soon, I began just winding some around a hook in various ways, and the Yarny finally emerged. Yarny is constructed solely of Glo-Bug yarn with either a hot-pink body and chartreuse topknot, or a chartreuse body and a hot-pink topknot. I'm sure that a red hook or a pink glow-

in-the-dark hook adds a lot to the fly's success as well.

The Yarny is probably the most durable of all the flies I use for sockeye, as long as the material is wrapped extremely tightly around the hook so it doesn't fray too much. Some head cement would undoubtedly keep it from fraying at all, but I rather like it bushy. It's so easy to tie that I can turn out enough for a trip in just one sitting.

Hook
Daiichi red or Gamakutsu #02609-P dark octopus hooks 2553 (size 4-3/0)

Thread
UNI-thread 6/0 red or fuchsia

Body
A small, flat piece of fuchsia Glo-Bug yarn tightly wound around the back half of the hook, followed by a tuft of fluorescent green Glo-Bug yarn protruding from the top of the hook, with more fuchsia Glo-Bug yarn wrapped tightly around the front of the hook. Or reverse the colors for a different version of the fly.

Playing a 12-pound salmon on an 8-weight fly rod.

STOP LIGHT

The Stop Light is one of my own Cactus Chenille inventions for Pacific salmon. It is particularly effective for both chums and silvers and, if tied large enough, also for kings. When Cactus Chenille appeared in fly shops, I was probably one of the first people to buy it. I simply couldn't resist. I could tell immediately that this was one synthetic material that was going to revolutionize salmon flies. I was right! This fantastic stuff has an allure that is absolutely irresistible to all five kinds of Pacific salmon, even sockeye (if you tie it very small).

The brilliant red color highlights the stiff, glistening material and makes his fly dazzlingly visible under water. The undulation and sheen of the spikes make for lots of action, too. Since red is a definite trigger color for fish, I started with it when designing this fly. Then, since the snowy-day white version of the material is really appealing to me, I added some of that just for fun. Although the fly really didn't need any additional sparkle or flash, I couldn't resist giving it some with bright Diamond Braid and Krystal Flash. The fish love it all.

Weight on the hook shank is optional, as is the bead or cone head, but both are advisable when you're planning on fishing in deeper, faster water. Stripping the Stop Light fast creates that zingy streak through the water that so often turns on silvers. Chums and kings also key in on this fly, and while you don't usually have to strip it as fast for them, you do need to have it moving. The Stop Light takes a little more time to tie than some of the other salmon flies, but it's worth it.

Hook
Daiichi 2441 (size 6-1/0) weighted and barb flattened to facilitate insertion into the bead or cone

Thread
UNI-thread 6/0 red

Bead/Cone
As desired for weight and appearance and attached before tying the body of the fly

Tail
A clump of red Krystal Flash mixed with red Flashabou about the length of the hook shank

Body
Red Diamond Braid wrapped along 2/3 of the length of the hook shank, followed by two wraps of white Cactus Chenille and two wraps of red Cactus Chenille up to right behind the cone or bead

Wing
A clump of red Krystal Flash mixed with red Flashabou about the length of the hook shank

Collar
A webby, red saddle hackle tied in by the butt and wrapped as a collar

Children's salmon fishing boat at Orca Adventure Lodge in Cordova, Alaska.

GO LIGHT

While I began creating the Go Light and its ruby sister the Stop Light, it was the Go Light that I initially tied the most so that I could try them out in one of the rivers in Alaska where I know that the fish are partial to green. I had guessed right, and silvers took them with abandon. Initially I didn't include the white Cactus Chenille wraps in the Go Light though because I didn't think that it would particularly enhance the fly. But, when I finally did add it, not only could I see the fly better in the water, but so, I believe, could the fish.

Initially, I tied both the Stop and the Go on long-shanked size 2 salmon-fly hooks because the design seemed to lend itself to the silhouette of a baitfish, but now I find that I sometimes tie them in smaller sizes as well. The silvers and chums seem to like both the small and large versions, but kings seem to prefer the large style. I thought perhaps a smaller fly might be more appealing to pink and sockeye salmon, but that didn't prove to be the case. These aren't their favorite flies no matter what size they are. Obviously, not

every species of salmon likes all of the same type, color, or size, of the various flies that we present to them.

The Go Light is fished the same way as the Stop Light, usually with fast strips. Sometimes I alternate fishing with the two colors just to see if one will take more fish than the other. It's still a little early to have very convincing results from my unscientific research, but, pretty much, it appears to be a draw.

Hook
Daiichi 2441 (size 6-1/0) weighted and barb flattened to facilitate insertion into the bead or cone

Thread
UNI-thread 6/0 green

Bead/Cone
As desired for weight and appearance and attached before tying the body of the fly

Tail
A clump of green Krystal Flash mixed with green Flashabou about the length of the hook shank

Body
Green Diamond Braid wrapped along 2/3 of the length of the hook shank, followed by two wraps of white Cactus Chenille and two wraps of green Cactus Chenille up to right behind the cone or bead

Wing
A clump of green Krystal Flash mixed with green or chartreuse Flashabou about the length of the hook shank

Collar
A webby green or chartreuse saddle hackle tied in by the butt and wrapped as a collar

Measuring a bright "jack" king salmon on the Naknek River, Alaska.

CLOUSER MINNOW

Bob Clouser, creator of Clouser Minnow, calls this the "fly for all species." I got introduced to it on a saltwater fly-fishing trip to Mexico and felt as if I'd discovered a gold mine. Large versions caught tuna and more while smaller varieties caught everything swimming inshore. Naturally, I came right back to Alaska and tried them with all of our fish species. Clouser was right! The Clouser Minnow is definitely a "must-have" pattern for your Pacific salmon fly boxes. I tie and use Clousers in virtually all my salmon fishing, except for sockeye. There's just something about it that is so "right" that at times I think it may rival the Egg Sucking Leech as the one fly with which you could fish for all of Alaska's Salmon. Forced to choose between the two for a one-fly

contest in the northland, I'd be hard pressed to decide.

Basic dumbbell lead eyes are standard for this fly, but I have experimented a little with other types and weights of eyes. While some of them do all right, the fly just doesn't seem to perform quite as well without the heavy ones. You can fish this great fly either with long, steady strips, with an up-and-down jigging motion, or with a short, quick "popcorn" action. All work well for me. I stick with a size 2 hook for silvers and chums but go larger for kings and smaller for pinks. A size 6 or 4 pink-and-white Clouser is a home-run hitter for pink salmon.

Hook
Daiichi 2546 or X452 (size 6-2/0)

Thread
UNI-thread 6/0 in color to match the body

Eyes
Dumbbell lead, heavy Spirit River Real Eyes Plus, Presentation Eyes, Pseudo Eyes, or painted lead eyes as desired for weight and appearance and attached before tying the body of the fly

Bottom Wing
Usually white bucktail

Flash
Flashabou in a color to match or contrast with wing

Top Wing
Sparse bundle of olive, tan, blue or other bucktail in the color of your preference

The author releasing an Alaska Peninsula fish.

A great, but buggy, day of fishing on the Alaska Peninsula.

TINY TIM

Another of the small, short-shanked flies that sockeye salmon take so readily, this one also appeals to silver and sometimes pink salmon as well. I like to use the red hooks for many of these flies, because I think that it adds a somewhat different dimension to the finished fly. The purple and red contrast in Tiny Tim's materials really appeals to me, and I figured it would also appeal to the fish. I'm always experimenting with different combinations of Diamond Braid for bodies and multicolor Krystal Flash for wings or tails, but the pearl Flashabou with its visible glow is what really sets this fly apart. Since I am partial to hackle collars, I gave one to Tim, one night when I was tying, and thought he looked pretty spiffy.

Tim is best fished dead drift for sockeye, except where the current is so swift that it sweeps him right past the fish before they have time to get a good look at him. You can slow him down with a small split shot on the leader, or some lead on the shank under the body, or both. Especially when they are holding in slow, shallow water on a bright, sunny day, silvers often favor this fly

over other, larger offerings, too. Even chum salmon go for them from time to time. Tims are another one of the small flies that can easily get lost in your fly box. Don't let it happen. You'll be hunting for them when you're out with the sockeye.

Some fish Tim on the dangle, and some use long, slow strips to give the Flashabou maximum time to get the attention of the fish. Many different approaches seem to bring success with this little fellow.

Hook
Daiichi red octopus hook 2553 (size, 6-2)

Thread
UNI-thread 6/0 red

Tail
A short clump of pearl Flashabou no longer than hook shank

Body
Purple or blue Diamond Braid

Wing
Several strands of multi-colored Krystal Flash

Collar
Webby red saddle hackle tied in by the butt and wrapped as a collar

Loading up to go salmon fishing in Lake Clark National Park, Alaska.

PINKIE-GREENIE

Don't be mistaken, this stubby, weird-looking little creation of mine is really a simple marvel in disguise. Easy to tie, and easy to cast and fish, this fly will take more Pacific salmon than you can imagine. It has everything: the right material, the attention-getting eyeballs, a perky little tail, and, if you like, red or glow-in-the-dark hooks that seem to have such appeal to salmon.

Another among the many Pacific salmon flies using Cactus Chenille, this one is so ugly it's cute. It makes no pretense at all that it is anything else. But, once you use it, it quickly makes a believer out of you.

Tied un-weighted and with the pair of nickel or plastic eyes, the Pinkie-Greenie will drift right into the mouth of a sockeye, if you use the basic technique of getting the fly to the mouth level of the fish and staying in touch with the feel of it to sense the hook-up when it occurs. It will also quickly get stuck in the jaw of a silver, chum, or king salmon when tied larger with heavier eyes and/or more weight

and stripped either long and steady, or short and jerky. Pink salmon seem to like it just a bit more weighted than you'd tie to fish for sockeye, but with the same action you'd use with the other three species.

The fun of this fly is that you can easily turn it into a Greenie-Pinkie, or the Greenie-Orangie, or the Greenie-Purplie, or the Pinkie-Whitie, or the Purplie-Pinkie, and so on. Switch out the tail for a different color and/or for marabou or hackle if you want to. They all work, ugly or not.

Hook
Daiichi red octopus hook 2553 or Mustad 92569NP-FC (Neon Beak hooks) (size 4-1/0) weighted or un-weighted

Thread
UNI-thread 6/0 in pink, red, or chartreuse

Eyes
Spirit River Real Eyes in gold or nickel to match the size of the hook and attached before tying the body of the fly

Tail
Pink or chartreuse body fur half the length of the hook shank

Rear body
Pink or chartreuse wrapped on rear half of hook shank

Front body
Chartreuse or pink wrapped around the eyes and the front half of the hook shank

Sockeye salmon fishing from an anchored-up drift boat in July on the Kenai River in Alaska.

FIREWALL

The Firewall is another of my designs that was created specifically to capitalize on the silver salmon's love of the color fuchsia. They just can't seem to get enough of it. One night when I was sitting at my tying table, I looked down and realized that all of the materials lying there in front of me were hot pink. I started combining them in different ways, and the Firewall was the result.

The red or glow-in-the-dark short-shanked hooks, fuchsia Flashabou, and eyeballs were the original materials that made up this fly. At first I tied the entire fly with only those, but later I decided that the Glo-Bug yarn tail made a fly with a much better silhouette. Even better, I now had two dissimilar types of material for different movement in the current. It works like gangbusters.

You can replicate the fly with a wide variety of other colors and color combinations because even silvers want something different once in a while. I've seen them turn completely off to a fly that they have been hammering all morning when

the light suddenly changes. It usually takes a while before they turn back on. Chums also like the pattern, but they are not so prone to turning off and turning on. Tied in larger sizes, the Firewall also appeals to kings, and, because it's pink, you can expect that the pink salmon will eat it up, too. Sockeye also take it occasionally if tied on a smaller, un-weighted hook with or without eyes.

Hook
Daiichi red/fuchsia octopus hook 2553 or Mustad 92569NP-FC Neon Beak hook (size 6-1/0) un-weighted

Thread
UNI-thread 6/0 red or hot pink

Eyes
Red Presentation or Pseudo eyes to match the hook size, tied on a little bit back of the hook eye and attached before tying the body of the fly

Tail
A tuft of hot-pink Glo-Bug yarn adorned with the tips of about fifteen or twenty strands of red or hot-pink Flashabou on top

Body/Wing
The remainder of the strands of red or hot-pink Flashabou that were used for the tail, wrapped tightly around the hook and around the eyes with remainder of the tips pointed upright behind the eyes as a stubby wing

Releasing a fresh sockeye salmon on a remote beach on Kodiak Island, Alaska.

MARDI GRAS

This fly came about when I saw Flashabou Weave in the fly shop and simply couldn't wait until I had created a fly with it. The mix of fuchsia, purple, pink, and gold strands was absolutely irresistible. It wasn't quite as flashy as the regular Flashabou colors were, but I reasoned it would have more appeal to fish resting in low, clear water.

The original was a single-material fly. I just made a rope of about twenty strands of the Flashabou Weave, tied about a half-inch of it on as a tail, wrapped the remainder tightly around the hook, and left the tips attached for a wing. Bingo! They worked great. In order to make sure that wasn't just a fluke, I tied up a bunch of them and took them on one of my silver salmon trips and had my clients be field-testers. They, too really scored. Later I asked one woman if she'd like to change patterns. Her emphatic answer was, "Don't touch this fly."

That night, I told the group they had to name the fly, and it took several bottles of wine for them to reach consensus. When one of the women,

who was from New Orleans, said that the fly looked to her just like a big, wild party, the words Mardi Gras popped out. And the rest is history!

Since then I've come to decorate the basic Mardi Gras with eyeballs, cones, beads, hackle collars, marabou tails, wings, and more. These embellished flies also catch fish like crazy, but don't leave home without some originals, too.

ORIGINAL

Hook
Daiichi 2441 (size 4-1/0) weighted

Thread
UNI-thread 6/0

Tail
The tips of 15 or 20 strands of Flashabou Weave #1348 3-strand blend of red/purple/gold about one-half the length of the hook shank

Body/Wing
The remainder of the strands of Flashabou Weave wrapped as a rope and wound tightly around the hook shank, with the tips left loose and tied back as a wing

ENHANCED

Hook
Daiichi 2441 (size 4-1/0) weighted with barb flattened to facilitate insertion of a bead or cone

Bead/Cone/Eyes
As desired for weight and appearance and inserted onto the hook, and tied on prior to the completion of the remainder of the fly

Tail/Body/Wing
As the original except for the addition of a tuft of purple or hot-pink marabou tied in for a tail and/or a wing

Collar
Webby saddle hackle tied in by the butt and wrapped as a collar

SPARKLER

The Sparkler is one of those effective flies that I can tie lots of quickly for my clients. Once you start tying with beads, cones and eyeballs, you'll begin to see how useful they are in giving a fly a certain look, plus some extra weight. You'll probably find that you are using them a lot. More and more of the Pacific salmon flies I tie sport one of the three. The same thing pretty much goes for hackle collars that I use to fill up the hole that usually forms behind them.

The Sparkler is just a bead, cone or eyeballs, a mix of contrasting colors of Flashabou, and a saddle-hackle collar. Fushcia and gold are the two colors that make up most of my Sparklers. Over time though, I've learned to use less-gaudy colors to please silvers that are farther away from salt water or ones that may be in shallower, slower water where a too-bright fly often spooks them. A blue/green combination is usually successful as are purple and gold and blue and gold.

The appeal of the Sparkler has to be all the fluttering color in the Flashabou that the fish sees in the water. Add to that the waving strands of hackle from the collar, and you've got one heck of a good attractor. Remember, that's all that most of our salmon flies really are. They seldom imitate a specific food source. Instead, they are just mostly big, gaudy, attention-getting streamers. Much of the time they fish like streamers as well.

Hook
Daiichi 2441 (size 4-2/0) with barb flattened to facilitate the insertion on a bead or a cone

Bead/Cone/Eyes
As required for weight and appearance and tied on prior to the completion of the remainder of the fly

Wing
Twenty-five or more strands of two different colors of Flashabou just a little longer than the shank of the hook and tied in behind the bead

Collar
Webby saddle hackle tied in by the butt and wrapped as a collar

Note: Try color combinations of green/purple, fuchsia/gold, silver/blue, etc.

A pair of silver salmon fresh from Prince William Sound, Alaska.

  Pacific Salmon Flies

ARTICULATED BUNNY LEECH

Articulated flies have become popular in both freshwater and saltwater fishing over the last few years. The pronounced wiggle they create in the water is absolutely irresistible to most fish. Many people believe that placing the hook at the end of an elongated fly also helps to avoid short strikes.

Anglers must be careful to check the fishing regulations when fishing with articulated flies. Many fisheries restrict terminal tackle to a single hook. Usually, it's easier to remove the front hook and bend after tying the fly than it is to always have pliers strong enough to cut a size 4 or 2 hook with you on the river.

Rabbit strips have become the component of choice for many articulated leech patterns. It's a proven fish-catching material, and its thickness makes it ideal for forming the connection between the two hooks.

The type and length of the connector, together with the way the fly is stripped through the water, are what makes the rear of the fly wiggle. A slow, jigging strip can get the tail of the fly flopping up and down with pronounced vigor, while a long, slow strip can make it wave in more of a sideways motion out at the tip of the fly. Some tiers also weight the front section of articulated flies for use in deeper water.

Hook #1
This will be the rear hook on the finished fly: Daiichi 2441 or 2546/X452 (size 4-1/0) weighted or un-weighted

Thread
UNI-thread 6/0 in color to match the other materials

Tail
One and one-half to two inches of the tip of a straight-cut black bunny strip tied in skin-side down together with three or four strands of multi-colored Krystal Flash (this helps disguise the connection between the two hooks)

Body
The remainder of the straight-cut black bunny strip palmered tightly around the hook shank and tied off at the head

Wing
Multi-colored Krystal Flash

Connection
About six inches of 30-pound fly-line backing looped through and around the eye of Hook #1. (Remove Hook #1 from the vise) Backing will be tied onto the shank of hook #2 when it is inserted into the vise.

Hook #2
This is the front hook on the finished fly: Daiichi 2441 or 2546/X452 (size 4-1/0) weighted or unweighted with barb flattened to facilitate insertion of a bead or cone head

Bead/Cone/Eyes
Gold, silver, copper, or bead-chain, lead, or plastic as desired for weight and appearance and attached before tying the body of the fly

Connection
Insert Hook #2 into the vise and lay the fly-line backing from Hook #1 onto its shank with a 1/2-inch gap between the two hooks to ensure that the back of the finished fly will flop around. Then wrap the backing down completely along the shank of Hook #2.

Tail
One and one-half to two inches of the tip of another straight-cut black bunny strip tied in skin-side down with three or four strands of multicolored Krystal Flash (this tip helps disguise the connection between the two hooks)

Body
The remainder of the straight-cut black bunny strip palmered tightly around the hook shank up to the bead head

Wing
A few strands of multicolored Krystal Flash

Collar
Optional. If used, webby black or contrasting color saddle hackle tied in by the butt and wrapped as a collar

SPOOK

I created this fly one dark and windy night when the ghosts were out and about. It seemed to me that the opalescent, pearly blue color made this gorgeous fly absolutely other-worldly. Its light-refraction qualities are beyond any other materials I tie with. Not quite white, and not quite blue, with just a touch of pale green, its look in the water is amazing. It mirrors the fluid colors of the moving river at the same time it emits a radiance that focuses all our attention right on it. And that goes for the fish's attention as well.

Even though the original fly is still my favorite, I sometimes tie this fly all in pearly white or some of the other pale Glisten Gloss colors with the pearl Flashabou in the tail. The palest of shell pink material produces a real pink-attractor fly too.

After a down-and-across cast, I slide the Spook slowly along, well within the cone of vision of the fish, and am always amazed how many heads move to take a closer look. Silvers will often accelerate to strike

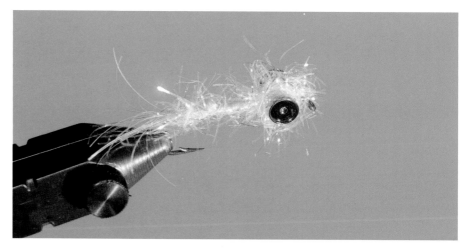

when a slowly-moved fly suddenly seems to dart away from them, so a quick increase in speed when the fish moves toward the fly can sometimes do the trick.

All of the salmon species seem attracted to this fly tied in different sizes. Even sockeye, those that refuse to chase salmon, sometimes take the small-sized Spooks. Often just letting the fly hang in the current is all that's necessary to get a hook-up. Other times stripping fast can make the fly look like a streak of lightning piercing the night sky.

Hook
Daiichi 1720 or Mustad 9672 (size 4-1/0) usually un-weighted

Thread
UNI-thread 6/0 in white or very light blue

Eyes
Spirit River silver nickel, bead-chain, or white-painted dumbbell eyes as desired for weight and appearance and attached before tying the body of the fly

Tail
Short clump of pale, blue-green Flashabou #36963 and one wrap of Estaz Grande Glissen Gloss, Opalescent Light Blue

Body
Approximately 15 strands of pale blue-green Flashabou made into a rope and wrapped tightly around the middle of the hook (fewer strands of Flashabou will be required on smaller hook sizes)

Head
Estaz Grande Glisten Gloss Opalescent Light Blue wrapped around the eyes and tied off right behind them

Heading out for some silver salmon fishing in Prince William Sound, Alaska.

PINK POLLYWOG

Believe it or not, the funny-looking Pink Pollywog is the prime example of a few patterns that actually induce some Pacific salmon species to take a fly on the surface. Known as "the Wog" in Alaska, this abomination really, truly, does work, just not all the time and just not for all five species.

The Wog is a large, hair waker fly fished much like a bass popper. A real pain to cast because of its wind-resistance, it really goes to work when skated or waked along in the water, interspersed with a series of twitches, gurgles, or pops to get the fish's attention. Cast directly down-stream of you and then bring the fly back, stripping *erratically* and lifting your rod tip against the resistance of the current. A strong side-arm cast often works best for getting this fly to the fish, and heavier leaders help the fly turn over. Wogs lose buoyancy quickly, so douse the deer-hair body with softened floatant before fishing them.

Silver salmon are the primary target for the fly, but chum and pinks are also known to grab it. Conditions must be right for success with the Wog, however. It is most effective in fairly shallow water with little or no current, and a good concentration of fish. The distinct bulge in the water just behind the fly is the signal you've got a follower. When you do, speed-up your stripping to induce the take. Watching the huge, bulb-nose of a buck-silver inhaling your Wog is something you'll never forget. If you don't know the two-handed retrieve used in salt-water fly-fishing, learn it immediately, or you won't be successful in hooking up with Wogs. The more rapidly the fly moves, the more the fish like it.

Hook
Tiemco 8089 (size 2) unweighted

Thread
UNI-thread 6/0 in a color to match the other materials

Tail
Large clump of fluffy marabou as long as the hook shank with a few strands of purple, blue, pearl or other Flashabou colors for contrast

Body
Clumps of deer hair, usually, pink, but also can be orange or chartreuse, packed tightly along the hook shank and then trimmed to desired shape

Wings
Trimmed deer hair, as with the body

Chasing a wog near Nome, Alaska.

HOT LIPS

I first saw the Hot Lips in a fly shop in Anchorage many years ago. Everyone was examining it carefully, quite unconvinced that it would really catch silvers as one fellow was claiming. Still, I bought a couple to try since I was off on a silver salmon fishing trip a few days later.

I wasn't very skilled at fishing Hot Lips initially. But, late the first afternoon, as I accidently stripped it quickly and sloppily back towards me getting ready to make another cast, a large salmon snout suddenly appeared right behind it. I was so flabbergasted I nearly dropped my rod. Maybe this thing really did work, I marveled as I took a few minutes to analyze what I had been doing that had piqued the fish's interest. A few more extra-fast and messy retrieves against the current later, I finally had a large silver hooked-up. Clearly, this wasn't just any old streamer but a whole new approach to salmon fishing on a fly rod.

Most people describe fishing the Hot Lips as being the same way that a bass angler fishes poppers—lots of noise, lots of action, and lots of speed. Buck silver salmon are the most eager

dry-fly chasers, by far. I'm convinced that all the action, combined with the male fish's competitiveness as it nears spawning, trigger its chase instinct for such topwater flies. The fly works best in water that is crowded with fish and is neither too deep nor too fast. Once they see it, they're on it. They won't stay on it, however, if you slow down your retrieve once they're interested. Speed it up as though it is getting away and you'll often trigger the strike. Try Hot Lips in fuchsia, orange, or yellow, too.

Hook
Daiichi 2441 (size 2)

Thread
UNI-thread 6/0 hot pink

Tail
A mix of chartreuse and white or hot-pink and white marabou as long as the hook shank with a few strands of pearl Flashabou

Body
Medium or large chartreuse or hot-pink Cactus Chenille

Wing and Lips
Half-inch-wide chartreuse or hot-pink closed-cell fly foam tied in at rear and stretched over the shank and then over and under the hook eye and tied off. Cut the foam in two in front of the hook-eye to form the lips and trim to shape

Note: Some versions of this fly use a foam strip on both the top and bottom of the hook shank and trim the foam in front of the hook-eye to form the lips.

Fishing a sockeye salmon lake on the Alaska Peninsula, all alone.

Chugach State Park

BEST FLIES FOR EACH SALMON SPECIES

FLY NAME	KING SALMON (color/size)	PINK SALMON (color/size)	
Everglow	Chartreuse, orange, or pink (size 2-3/0)	Chartreuse, orange, or pink (size 6-4)	
Bunny-Winged Salmon Leech	Fushcia, purple, white, chartreuse, or orange (size 4-2/0)		
Little Red Riding	Red (size 4-1/0)		
Flash Fly	Red/silver, chartreuse/silver, or purple/gold (size 2-3/0)		
Fish Candy	Hot-pink, orange, chartreuse, white, or purple (size 6-3/0)	Hot-pink, orange, chartreuse, white, or purple (size 6-8)	
Rajah	Pink/silver or chartreuse/silver (size 4-1/0)		
Purple Egg Sucking Leech	Purple, black, white, or chartreuse (size 2-3/0)	Purple (size 4-6)	
Sockeye Orange		Orange/black (size 6-4)	
Lemon Fly-Fushcia/Fuchsia	Hot-pink, orange chartreuse, white or glow-in-the-dark colors (size 6-4)	Hot-pink, orange, chartreuse, white or glow-in-the-dark colors (size 6-4)	
Bead-Head Electric Leech	Black, purple, orange, pink, or chartreuse (size 4-3/0)		
Starlight Leech	Black, purple, or chartreuse (size 2-3/0)		
Nothing Fly		Hot-pink (size 6-4)	
Red Hot	Red or fuchsia (size 2-4/0)		
Flesh Fly/Bunny Fly	Fushcia, purple, orange black, chartreuse, or tan (size 2-3/0)		
Comet	Orange/gold, pink/gold, or chartreuse/gold (size 4-3/0)	Orange/gold, pink/gold, or chartreuse/gold (size 4-8)	
Purple Performer			
Fat Freddy	Hot-pink, hot orange, or chartreuse (size 2-3/0)		
Popsicle	Pink/orange, pink/purple, or chartreuse/orange (size 4-3/0)		
Blue Skies		Baby blue/white (size 6-8)	
Yarny	Hot-pink/chartreuse (size 2-3/0)		
Stop Light	Red/white (size 4-3/0)		
Go Light	Green/white (size 4-3/0)		

SOCKEYE SALMON (color/size)	CHUM SALMON (color/size)	COHO SALMON (color/size)
	Chartreuse, orange, or pink (size 2-3/0)	Chartreuse, orange, or pink (size 2-3/0)
		Fushcia, purple, white, chartreuse, or orange (size 4-1/0)
	Red (size 4-1/0)	Red (size 4-1/0)
	Red/silver, chartreuse/silver, or purple/gold (size 2-1/0)	Red/silver, chartreuse/silver, or purple/gold (size 2-1/0)
Hot-pink, orange, chartreuse, white, or purple (size 6-8)	Hot-pink, orange, chartreuse, white,or purple (size 6-2)	Hot-pink, orange, chartreuse, white, or purple (size 6-2)
	Pink/silver or chartreuse/silver (size 4-1/0)	Pink/silver or chartreuse/silver (size 4-1/0)
	Purple, black, white or chartreuse (size 2-3/0)	Purple, black, white, or chartreuse (size 2-3/0)
Orange/black (size 6-4)		Orange/black (size 6-4)
	Hot pink, orange, chartreuse white or glow-in-the-dark (size 6)	Black, purple, orange, pink, or chartreuse (size 4-1/0)
	Black, purple, or chartreuse (size 2-1/0)	Black, purple, or chartreuse (size 2-1/0)
Hot-pink (size 6-4)		Hot-pink (size 6-4)
Red or fuchsia (size 2-6)	Red or fuchsia (size 2-1/0)	Red or fuchsia (size 2-1/0)
	Fushcia, purple, orange, black, chartreuse, or tan (size 2-1/0)	Fushcia, purple, orange, black, chartreuse, or tan (size 2-1/0)
Orange/gold, pink/gold, or chartreuse/gold (size 4-8)	Orange/gold, pink/gold, or chartreuse/gold (size 4-1/0)	Orange/gold, pink/gold, or chartreuse/gold (size 4-1/0)
Purple (size 6-4)	Purple (size 6-2)	Purple (size 6-2)
	Pink/orange, pink/purple, or chartreuse/orange (size 4-1/0)	Pink/orange, pink/purple, or chartreuse/orange (size 4-1/0)
Baby blue/white (size 6-8)		Baby blue/white (size 6-2)
Hot-pink/chartreuse (size 4-6)		Hot-pink/chartreuse (size 2-1/0)
	Red/white (size 4-1/0)	Red/white (size 4-1/0)
	Green/white (size 4-1/0)	Green/white (size 4-1/0)

BEST FLIES FOR EACH SALMON SPECIES

FLY NAME	KING SALMON (color/size)	PINK SALMON (color/size)	
Clouser Minnow	Pink/white, olive/white, or tan/white (size 2-3/0)		
Tiny Tim		Blue and white (size 6-4)	
Pinkie-Greenie	Pink/green, and other combinations (size 4-3/0)	Pink/green, and other combinations (size 4-2)	
Firewall	Red/fushcia (size 4-3/0)		
Mardi Gras	Red/orange/gold, or blue/black (size 2-3/0)		
Sparkler	Fushcia/gold, purple/gold, or blue/green (size 4-3/0)		
Articulated Bunny Leech	Black, fuchsia, purple, chartreuse, white, or tan (size 2-3/0)		
Spook	Light blue/pale blue-green (size 2-3/0)		
Pink Pollywog		Pink (size 4-2)	
Hot Lips		Pink or chartreuse (size 4-2)	

SOCKEYE SALMON (color/size)	CHUM SALMON (color/size)	COHO SALMON (color/size)
	Pink/white, olive/white, or tan/white (size 2-3/0)	Pink/white, olive/white, or tan/white (size 2-3/0)
Blue and white (size 6-4)		Blue and white (size 6-2)
Pink/green, and other combinations (size 4-2)	Pink/green, and other combinations (size 4-2)	Pink/green, and other combinations (size 4-2)
	Red/fushcia (size 4-1/0)	Red/fushcia (size 4-1/0)
	Red/orange/gold or blue/black (size 2-1/0)	Red/orange/gold, or blue/black (size 2-1/0)
	Fushcia/gold, purple/gold, or blue/green (size 4-1/0)	Fushcia/gold, purple/gold, or blue/green (size 4-1/0)
		Black, fuchsia, purple, chartreuse, white, or tan (size 2-1/0)
	Light blue/pale blue-green (size 2-1/0)	Light blue/pale blue-green (size 2-1/0)
	Pink, orange or chartreuse (size-2)	Pink, orange or chartreuse (size 2)
	Pink or chartreuse (size-2)	Pink or chartreuse (size-2)

Prince William Sound, Pink salmon caught on an egg fly in, fall.

About the Author

Cecilia "Pudge" Kleinkauf, a retired
university professor and attorney, has
owned and operated her instruction and
guide service, Women's Flyfishing,®
for over twenty-five of the forty-plus
years she has lived and fished in Alaska.
During that time she has introduced
countless women and couples to the
joys of fly-fishing all around Alaska
for salmon, trout, grayling, char, and
pike, as well as to saltwater locations in
Mexico, and other destination fisheries in
Argentina and Sweden.

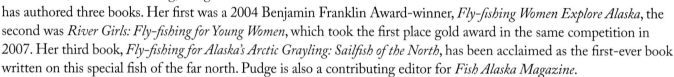

Together with her photographic
collaborator, Michael DeYoung, Pudge
has authored three books. Her first was a 2004 Benjamin Franklin Award-winner, *Fly-fishing Women Explore Alaska*, the
second was *River Girls: Fly-fishing for Young Women*, which took the first place gold award in the same competition in
2007. Her third book, *Fly-fishing for Alaska's Arctic Grayling: Sailfish of the North*, has been acclaimed as the first-ever book
written on this special fish of the far north. Pudge is also a contributing editor for *Fish Alaska Magazine*.

Women's Flyfishing® is a member of Trout Unlimited's Outfitters, Guides, and Business Members Program, and
of the Guides Association of the Federation of Fly-Fishers. Pudge is a member of the Alaska Fly-Fishers, TU, and
FFF, and is also one of the founding members of the International Women Fly-fishers. A pro staff for several fly-
fishing companies, Pudge is a featured "Explorer" on the *Alaska Magazine Television* series showing on PBS television.

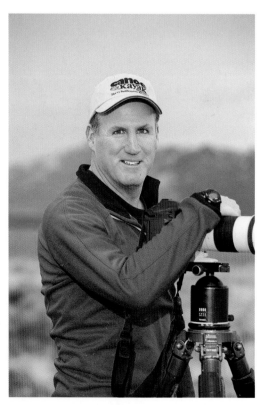

About the Photographer

Named "Master of Outdoor Lifestyle" by Digital Photo Pro Magazine
Michael DeYoung is a commercial photographer, adventurer, and
workshop instructor. He specializes in adventure and landscape
photography for advertising and editorial clients.

The former longtime Alaskan has photographed extensively for the
Alaska tourism industry and spent months on adventures of his own
throughout Alaska and the Yukon.

DeYoung's images appear regularly in national calendars,
magazines, catalogs, visitor guides and many other places. He has
photographed three other books with author Pudge Kleinkauf.

Michael and his wife and business partner, Lauri, live and run their
business in a sustainable home office powered 100% by solar energy
near the ski town of Taos, New Mexico.